YOUR GLORIOUS ENDEAVOR

YOUR GLORIOUS ENDEAVOR

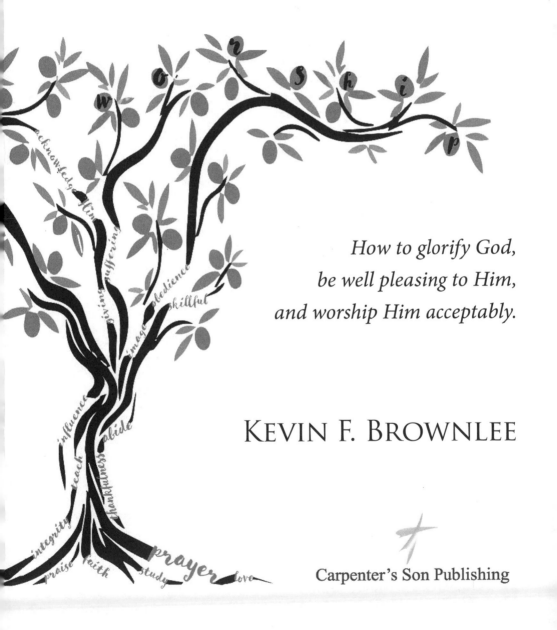

How to glorify God,
be well pleasing to Him,
and worship Him acceptably.

KEVIN F. BROWNLEE

Carpenter's Son Publishing

Published by Carpenter's Son Publishing, Franklin, Tennessee
Published in association with Larry Carpenter of Christian Book Services, LLC
www.christianbookservices.com

Unless otherwise noted, all Scripture quotations are from the New King James Version® of the Bible copyright © 1982 by Thomas Nelson, Inc. Used by permission. All rights reserved.

Scripture quotations marked (NLT) are taken from the Holy Bible, New Living Translation, copyright © 1996, 2004, 2007 by Tyndale House Foundation. Used by permission of Tyndale House Publishers, Inc., Carol Stream, Illinois 60188. All rights reserved.

Scripture quotations marked (NIV) are taken from the Holy Bible, New International Version®, NIV®. Copyright © 1973, 1978, 1984, 2011 by Biblica, Inc.™ Used by permission of Zondervan. All rights reserved worldwide. www.zondervan.com. The "NIV" and "New International Version" are trademarks registered in the United States Patent and Trademark Office by Biblica, Inc.

Cover Design by Kevin Brownlee and Suzanne Lawing
Interior by Adept Content Solutions
Edited by Gail Fallen
Printed in the United States of America
978-1-949572-61-2

www.yourgloriousendeavor.com
www.bluejeanschristian.com
kevin@bluejeanschristian.com

ACKNOWLEDGMENTS

Many people have impacted my life, and I would like to recognize a few with special thanks for their faithfulness to God and shaping this book:

My grandmother, Florence Sprinkle, who is in heaven now reasoning with God and her "pen pal" Dr. Francis Shaeffer. She's the Matriarch of our family, setting the bar high with a love for truth, godly intellectualism, and impacting on our world for Christ. She instituted my search and longing to glorify God.

My mother, Janet Brownlee, who I'm guessing has not quit hugging Jesus for over seventeen years now. You led me to our Lord as a young boy, and kept me close to Him with your daily prayers and influence. I still am in awe of your perseverance through unbelievable trials, and of your knowledge of the Bible, which I endeavor to emulate. This book is because of you. Oh, and making me listen to Dr. John MacArthur sermons on cassette during each of my drives to/from LeTourneau College and having to tell you three things I learned from each one was unbelievably brilliant. I now wish I hadn't complained so much. Thank you, Mom; I'm looking forward to seeing you again.

My dad, Fred Brownlee, who taught me the value of integrity, obedience, skillfulness, and being a positive influence on others shaped several chapters in this book. You also taught me and the importance and value of hard work, because God does. I love you, Dad.

My wife, Bunny, whose prayers and support are unmeasurable. Your godly respect, patience, and love are woven through the pages of this book, which would not be in print without you.

My daughter, Kallee, who taught me to replace my faults with love and grace and who is more like Jesus than many Christians I know.

My sister, Julie Peter, who gave me the confidence to write this book, and supported the endeavor with prayers and encouragement.

Pastor Landis Epp, who plowed ground and planted seeds in my life through twelve grade school years, hopefully this book gives you a little ride in the combine with a smile of glory to God.

Dr. Bryan Hughes, whose careful and precise sermon preparation, then delivery through expository preaching resulted in unbelievable notes and underlining in my Bible, which contributed immensely to this book, and because of you, God is glorified.

Dr. Chuck Missler, Dr. James MacDonald, and Dr. Charles Stanley whose teaching brought to me a love for God's Word and how to apply it in a practical way to my life for His glory.

CONTENTS

Your Glorious Endeavor

"Everyone who is called by My name, Whom I have
created for My glory; I have formed him, yes, I have
made him." (Isaiah 43:7, emphasis added)

"Therefore, whether you eat or drink, or whatever you do, do
all *to the glory of God*." (1 Corinthians 10:31, emphasis added)

Q. What is the chief end of man?
A. Man's chief end is to glorify God,
and to enjoy him forever.[1]

We all periodically ponder the question "What is the purpose of my life?" but satisfying answers elude most of us. What does grip us are feelings of uncertainty, inadequacy, or even disillusionment. People tell us life is more than eating, paying bills, taking kids to soccer, and watching TV, but that's all most of us seem to do. We "live for the weekend," but not much bigger than that.

"Other people," you say to yourself, "have exciting, fulfilling, purposeful lives; they make a difference in this world, but I'm not one of them."

You look around at your situation and ask, "How did I get here? This is less than I planned. Will it ever change?" You maintain a little hope that someday you'll know why you're here and plod along mostly looking downward on your path of life, waiting.

Couple that with a question we all know but never seek to answer: "Do I glorify God?" We are told in church we're supposed to glorify God yet have never actually heard how to do that. If we can do things that *don't* glorify God, it stands to reason there must be things we *can* do to glorify Him. It must be important, but no one specifically or even vaguely tells us how—even during all those Sunday mornings in church. So we assume God is not pleased with us because we don't know how to glorify Him the way He wants.

Could those questions be related? Is there an answer to satisfy both the questions of "What is my purpose in life?" and "How do I glorify God?" If so, the result would not only be life-changing, but our life would be incredibly full and abundant as Jesus promised in John 10:10! Instead of plodding along looking down and waiting for our life purpose, we can raise our eyes and know it *now*, and *do it now*! How thrilling!

The two scriptural verses at the beginning here say we have been created to glorify God. So our purpose in life as Christians is to glorify Him, and as 2 Corinthians 5:9 says, we should make it our aim to do so in a way that is well pleasing to Him. So how do we do that? What does it mean to glorify God, or bring glory to Him? What … *pleases* God?

It's taken me about thirty years, but I have come up with the answers! Based on Scripture, I've learned how to glorify God and wrote this book so you can too! We no longer have to hope we are doing it correctly or worry or if our job, our family, where we live, or even our hobbies are according to God's purpose for us: those are offshoots of glorifying God. We can even know how to *worship* God correctly!

First, before anything else, we must understand the meaning of the very interesting word "glory."

EXPLANATION OF THE WORD "GLORY"

The word "glory" occurs over four hundred times in the Bible and is used both as a noun (a thing or presence that can be seen), and as a verb (to glorify, an action). In the majority of occurrences, it is a noun describing God or something about Him, such as the overwhelming and majestic presence of God. The verb "glorify" occurs about twenty-six times in the Bible.

God's glory is described as a brilliant light, but it's much more than that. For example, when Moses wanted to see God in Exodus 33, he was told by God to hide behind a rock because of the brilliance of His glory and to only look on the back side of His glory after He passed by, for Moses' safety. Even after passing, when Moses looked, it bleached his hair white, and his skin shone for such a long time after, he had to wear a veil when talking to people! That gives us an idea of the magnitude of the noun version of the glory of God, so it stands to reason that the verb version must be something equally incredible and important to God. It is that *action* we have the privilege of doing! And this book will help you do just that.

There is no theme more central to the message of Scripture than the glory of God.
—Gerald Bray

In John 17, Jesus prayed for himself, His disciples, and for us. The theme of His prayer is twofold: unity, and glory. Unity of God the Father, Jesus, and us believers and the glory of God, Jesus, and us. God glorifying Jesus, Jesus glorifying God, and us believers glorifying God is a magnificent relationship circle, and our responsibility is to keep that circle going by bringing glory to God and Jesus.

I accepted Jesus as my Savior and Lord of my life over fifty years ago, and as long as I can remember, I have heard we are "to glorify God." I wanted to know how because it sounded important. I kept asking pastors and Bible teachers what that means ... and how do we do that. The answers were usually vague or overly simplistic. So I began keeping notes of whenever I heard the phrase, writing down the topic of the statement, and Bible passages if there were any.

I also kept notes when I came across something that brings glory to God while reading the Bible during my daily devotional time. After many years of this, I began compiling these ways to glorify God, whittling them down to unique and root ways, even to single words. Then, through several years of teaching this to adult Sunday school classes, at seminars, and even on a cruise ship, the results are in your very own hands: *sixteen specific things* to bring glory to God.

There are some very important statements you need to understand, though.

First, we do not have to perform these actions to gain or keep salvation or even righteousness. Ephesians 2:8–10 says, "For by grace you have been saved through faith, and that not of yourselves; it is the gift of God, not of works, lest anyone should boast. For we are His workmanship, created in Christ Jesus for good works, which God prepared beforehand that we should walk in them."

Salvation and righteousness are gifts from God to those of us who have accepted Jesus; we know He has already saved us from the penalty of our sins and made us righteous in the eyes of God, which is a gift! Romans 5:17 states that clearly where Paul wrote, "For if, because of one man's trespass, death reigned through that one man, much more will those who receive the abundance of grace and the free gift of righteousness reign in life through the one man Jesus Christ" (ESV).

Because of what Jesus did for us, we not only *want* to do things to glorify God as a "thank you" and out of obedience, but we should also remember that God prepared specific things beforehand for us *to* do. Yes, God, in His infinite wisdom, has given us some ways to say thanks! And you will discover those specific things as you read this book!

Second, Scripture is very clear: we are *not* to seek glory for ourselves, but seek it and give it to God. These are not things that elevate us, though they will make us a better Christian. We do these for love and for free.

These are things that bring glory to God, not us. Acts 12:23 says Herod was struck dead because he did not give glory to God, and in Acts 13:8–18 when God (through Paul) healed a crippled man, the people tried to give glory to Paul and Barnabas, who immediately tore their clothes and ran around crying out to the people not to give them glory, but to give it only to God.

Third, the gospel is paramount, and it's all about Jesus. What I mean by that is each way to glorify God is Bible based on and has at its core the good news of the gospel: Jesus came to the world to save lost sinners, and through Him alone, when we repent of our sins and believe in Jesus, we are saved and righteous before God. The ways to glorify God in this book all have the "aroma" of the gospel and have something to do with Jesus at the core and as the result.

In addition to that, each of these ways to glorify God actually improves our relationship with Jesus. The point of the Bible *is* Jesus. Its purpose is to point us to Jesus, and when you read and do these things to glorify God, your life will be emulating and pointing to Jesus more and more. So read on with that in mind, and you will be enriched by knowing Jesus more fully.

Whatever man may stand, whatever he may do, to whatever he may apply his hand—in agriculture, in commerce, and in industry, or his mind, in the world of art, and science—he is, in whatsoever it may be, constantly standing before the face of God. He is employed in the service of his God. He has strictly to obey his God. And above all, he has to aim at the glory of his God.
—Abraham Kuyper, Dutch statesman and theologian, 1837–1920

"ISN'T GLORIFYING GOD ANOTHER TERM FOR WORSHIP?"

So how do we obediently and effectively bring glory to God in these sixteen ways? And aren't these ways a form of worship toward God? It's very important to get this right: we owe that to God who *has* done so much for us, *is* doing so much for us, and *will* do so much more for us.

Most of us have heard of the following three ways to glorify God: Confession, praise, and worship. However, there are many more ways to glorify God than just those three. In fact, there are *sixteen* ways to glorify God that I have found. Worship is actually a summation of the sixteen and should be discussed on its own special level. We will do that at the conclusion of this book.

Sixteen ways may sound like a lot, I know, and maybe overwhelming, but they are really common everyday things we should do. They are things which can become sort of second nature to us or a way of life, and that, folks, is when our whole life becomes a glory to God! How awesome would that be?! That is also a way to worship Him!!

Now, as you read, you may think of other ways to glorify God, as I did, but the more I thought of those, the more I realized they can be boiled down to a more root form; yes, even to a single word ... one already on the "list." So if you think of another way to glorify God, first see if it has one of these sixteen as its root. If not, you can add it as another way!

I didn't include things we are supposed to be as a Christian. We glorify God by *doing* more than being. In other words, these ways are things we *do*, which brings more glory to Him than who or what we are. An example of something we are is *humble*, which we have to work on being or becoming as we go about our lives. We are never told in Scripture to be humble; we are told to humble *ourselves* … a result of something else such as when we *love* others or even when we are *thankful* (both of which are on this list). Another example is *forgiveness* … the root of forgiveness is love and image of Jesus. You will see that clearly when you read about love and image.

I want to reiterate that *doing* something to bring glory to God does just that … it glorifies Him. It doesn't glorify us, nor does it *improve our standing* with Him. Doing something or expressing something to or for Him doesn't make us righteous and doesn't make Him love us more—nor does it cause Him to need to bless us more as "payment for services rendered."

Repenting of our sins and living with Jesus as our Lord is enough. Jesus did everything else on the cross for us. Now, I am not advocating or teaching a "works-based religion." That would be taking something away from what Jesus did on the cross, or it would be adding something we have to do because Jesus didn't do a good enough or complete job. Both are completely incorrect. So it's important to do these things not because you have to or need to but because you *want* to. Do them because you love God and are thankful for what Jesus did for you … in fact, thank Jesus along the way for enabling these sixteen things to be voluntary, not a requirement.

"DOES GOD NEED US TO GLORIFY HIM?"

Does God need glory from us? Probably not—He's too "big." But *we* need to glorify Him! It helps us get to know Him and to serve Him. It is a win-win for us and for Him!

Before we get into the sixteen specific root words and how to implement them, we need to take a step back and look at the word "confession." We Christians have our own lingo sometimes, and this word is one of them. It is a double entendre: it has two meanings, and they both work for this topic of glorifying God:

1. Repentance of transgressions or sin
2. Proclaiming glory to God

Confession of Transgressions: The first one, repenting of your sins, *must happen before anyone can glorify God*. Because of the Holiness of God, any sin in our lives is like a barrier between us and God, and He cannot be glorified with that barrier in place. It's like a rock wall between us. There is, however, *one way* to smash that rock wall and get it out of the way (see John 14:6).

Confessing your sins and accepting the substitutionary payment of those sins by Jesus Christ is what removes that rock wall barrier. We have complete access to God thanks to what Jesus did for us on the cross. First John 1:9 says, "If we confess our sins, he is faithful and just to forgive us our sins and to cleanse us from all unrighteousness."

Scripture tells us that through Jesus, we have access in one Spirit to the Father (Eph. 2:18) in whom we have boldness and confident access through faith in Him (Eph. 3:12) to enter the holy place by the blood of Jesus (Heb. 10:19). In Him, we have redemption through His blood, the forgiveness of our sins, according to the riches of His grace (Eph. 1:7). Jesus said, "I am the way, and the truth, and the life; no one comes to the Father but through Me" (John 14:6).

It is by the grace of Jesus we can glorify God the Father ... and God sees, hears, and knows (which pleases Him) when we do. How cool is that!?

Confession as Proclamations: Once you have the confession of sins and forgiveness of them taken care of by Jesus, you can do this other type of confession: *proclaiming glory to God*. You do so in your thoughts, your words, and your actions. Those three are accomplished through using all of these ways to glorify God, which we will delve into deeply and unpack each to practical application in our lives:

- Prayer
- Faith (and Hope)
- Love
- Abide
- Obedience
- Acknowledge (Him)

- Integrity
- Skillful
- Influence
- Image
- Suffering
- Thankful
- Praise
- Giving
- Study
- Teach

You will discover something really amazing: Each of these somehow integrates with each other and complements each other! So keep an eye peeled and see if you can recognize those instances.

Then, we will appropriately end with *worship*. You will learn what it actually means (it means more than just singing), how to worship correctly, and how all sixteen of these are components of worship that glorifies God. Just as an automobile is a summation of all its parts, worship is a summation of the above sixteen parts, but you will see it is so much more! So hang in there, take your time, and remember each part is fun and fascinating in itself. When you're done, worshipping God correctly is like driving a Ferrari!

THE WARP AND WOOF (OR WEFT) OF GLORIFYING GOD

Because God is so incredible, so awesome, and so magnificent beyond our comprehension, glorifying Him must be equally incredible, awesome, magnificent, and beyond our ability to fully grasp. It might be, but I think we have to try. The "warp and woof" of this endeavor is to delve deeply into His Word, the Bible, and come up with things we can do to bring Him glory. From those scriptural passages, which are inspired by Him, we learn *of* Him as we learn how to bring glory *to* Him.

I use the term "warp and woof," which comes from the textile industry where the vertical threads of a garment are called the warp and the horizontal threads are the woof, for a reason. When we intertwine His Word (warp) with our best heartfelt efforts of application (woof), I believe God will be pleased with the "garment."

When I first heard that warp and woof term, I thought it had to do with dogs. So here is a dog analogy, if it interests you: A dog barking (woof) alone is noticeable and mostly negative and annoying, but barking for a trained reason (warp) is noticeable in a positive way and serves a purpose and is gratifying or comforting.

So there will be plenty of scriptural passages in this book as well as practical application, both of which *must go together* to adequately bring glory to God.

We can easily feel inadequate and too inferior to God to even attempt to glorify Him. However, God desires a personal relationship with each one of us, so much so that He sent His only Son to die on a cross so we can! I think because of that, we *must* glorify Him, and I also think He *wants* us to glorify Him! He gave us a "breadcrumb trail" to do so. That's pretty cool, as it's an open door between us and who sits on the throne of the universe. That open door is something He *wants* us to feel free to come through.

You know, after putting this list together and explaining how to execute each one, I am convinced we *must* do it. I can't help but think God will be proud of us and pleased with us for trying as He encourages us to enjoy the effort. I would encourage you to develop a *love* of glorifying God … and a *hatred* for anything that does not glorify Him. Let that become your *lifestyle* and, ultimately, your *purpose* in life!

The study of each of the sixteen ways is not an exhaustive oration of each, but it's certainly enough for normal people like you and me to get us "soundly going down the road" of glorifying God. This book is a vehicle of the power of God through which He is glorified by people.

THE PAPER-TOWEL TIE

Those of us who are parents can tell a story of the time one of our little preschool-aged children worked long and hard on a craft-type gift and presented it to us on our birthday, Christmas, or Mother's Day/Father's Day. Mine was tie made from a folded paper towel with crayon artwork, glitter shaken on squiggly lines of Elmer's Glue, confetti, and pieces of glued-on dried elbow macaroni.

Yours was probably something similar, and I'm sure you will recall it was far from perfect, but our child tried so hard, their intention and motivation were pleasing, and our hearts were warmed while our eyes teared up joyously. We were more than satisfied by our little person's effort.

Even if that's what the results of this book may seem like to God, you have to try: You will be much better for the effort, and warming His heart will be just fine.... His eyes may even tear up, pleased by your glorious endeavor! My prayer for you is that when you glorify God in these ways, you will actually glow with the glory of God—maybe not as Moses did, but enough so others around you will notice something glorious about you.

Albert Einstein said there's simplicity on the other side of complexity, so hang in there to the end, take as much time as you need to read through these, each a glorious endeavor in itself, and learning these is really important to us and to God. Each one of these sixteen pieces are a significant part of the paper-towel tie!

★ ★ ★

Please note: At the end of each chapter is a place for you to write in your own personal "Practical Applications" for that specific way to glorify God, and in each instance, I have helped you by giving the first one!

# 1 PRAYER

Prayer is having a conversation with God, the creator and sustainer of everything that exists. It's is an incredible privilege. We glorify God when we come to him in prayer. Prayer is the essential part of a relationship with God. God loves to hear from us, and we Christians have this opportunity because Jesus, on the cross, removed the barrier of sin that prevented our direct communication with God.

Up until a few thousand years ago, God "resided" in a certain place in the temple called the Holy of Holies. There was a tall curtain around the Holy of Holies separating people from God except for the high priest, who went in only once a year. Because God cannot be near sinful people, the curtain was a separation of protection. Isaiah 59:2 says our sins separate us from God, and only the high priest was allowed to communicate with God; regular people could not.

However, when Jesus died on the cross, that tall thick curtain was ripped open from top to bottom; in fact, God Himself tore it. You can read about this in Matthew 27:51. That torn and open curtain signifies that we, because of Jesus Christ, can now communicate with God whenever we want (Hebrews 10:19–20 confirms this). God is no longer in the Holy of Holies but goes out and dwells with His people, and we have access to

Him. In essence, we "have the ear of God" through prayer, so we should use that privilege and opportunity every chance we get.

2 Corinthians 6:16 tells us God said, *"I will dwell in them and walk among them. I will be their God, and they shall be my people."* That's fascinating, since prior to Jesus only select few people could pray to God, and if ordinary people wanted to repent of sins or pray to God, they had to tell the priest, who would do that for them once a year. So when Jesus' disciples saw Him praying, they asked if they could and *how.* (More on that later in the chapter.)

Prayer puts into perspective who God is and who we are. God isn't a genie existing to give us our wishes but is the creator and sustainer of the universe, whom we serve. God isn't your servant; you are His.

Prayer acknowledges God as God and the fact that we need Him. A lack of prayer sends the message we don't need Him and can succeed without Him. Prayer sends the message we *do* need Him and cannot succeed in the best way possible without Him.

Prayer has become so important to me that it's listed first in the series of "to-dos" of glorifying God. But I *really* wanted to list it first when I realized how important prayer was, even to Jesus. He prayed often, many times during tumultuous events, and even at the expense of sleep. In fact, when His disciples had an opportunity to ask Jesus a question, they didn't ask how He healed the sick and blind or raised people from the dead or fed over five thousand people from just five biscuits and a couple of little fish; they asked Him to teach them how to pray. Prayer needs to be *that* important to you too.

TYPES OF PRAYER

There are four types of prayer: formal, ritual, flare, and spontaneous. We should do all of them each day.

- *Formal* prayers are time alone with God as Jesus taught us in Matthew 6:9–13: It's not about reciting that prayer but using it as a blueprint or pattern to follow with our own words. We begin by repenting of any sins. Jesus took and paid the penalty for all of our sins, past, present, and future, but it's good to tell

God we know we messed up, are sorry about it, and will do our best to not repeat it. Confessing our sins and asking for forgiveness from God is sort of like cleaning up the room before we invite Him in for a chat. Then we may proceed in the manner Jesus laid out ... or at least something similar. This also includes intercessory prayer where we pray for others as well as ourselves. Formal prayer usually takes place when you're alone, with no interruptions, and preferably on your knees in humility and reverence to the almighty God.

- *Ritual* prayer is what we do at the beginning and end of our church service, or before we eat each meal. Psalm 55:17 says to pray "evening and morning and at noon" and God will hear you. This prayer type typically centers on the task or event at hand and always includes gratitude to Him.

- *Flare* prayer is when something stressful or tragic occurs and you send up a "flare" prayer for quick help. Here are some examples: You suddenly can't remember the answer to question 12 on your final exam. You're driving downhill, and your brakes fail. You see the trophy bull elk of your dreams on the final day of hunting season, and you have only one shot at him. Or you realize you are missing one ingredient in your recipe, and your dinner guests arrive in five minutes. In Psalm 50:15 God says we are to "Call upon Me in the day of trouble; and I will deliver you and you shall glorify Me." Remember to glorify Him when He answers.

- *Spontaneous* prayer is relating the things we see, do, or hear relative to Him as if He was a good friend spending the day with us next to us. Examples include "Lord, I sure appreciate that sunrise," or "Thank you, God, for letting me live among these beautiful mountains you created," or "Please help me with this phone call."

In 1 Thessalonians 5:17, Paul said to pray without ceasing. Ever wonder about that? We do this by involving all of these types of prayer throughout all of our day. God loves to communicate with us and loves to hear from us, and prayer is one way to glorify Him. Prayer sets our minds on what really matters and forces us to focus on God, thank Him, praise Him, and even worship Him … all of which glorifies Him.

Here's one good analogy of using these types of prayer during your day, each day: If your best friend spent the entire day with you, by your side the whole time, and you talked to your friend the same amount of time as you talk to God during a day, would he/she want to do it again the next day? Would your friend even stay your friend?

We tend to talk to God in prayer just before dinner, using the same few words, and just before we go to sleep (and we probably doze off prior to finishing). The average Christian spends less than thirty seconds praying per day … and barely does so once a day. That's terrible, folks, and God is not glorified. We can do a lot better than that. In fact, we need to do so much better that God *wants* to spend the day with us. You want that too. God is not a distant, mean "cosmic killjoy" but a near, loving Father who desires a communicative relationship with us.

"I TRY TO PRAY, BUT IT'S AWKWARD, AND I PROBABLY SOUND STUPID. "

Do any of your prayers sound like this? "Lord, I just, Lord, want you, Lord, to hear my prayer, Lord. Just be with me, Lord, and Lord just make your presence known, Lord, to me, Lord, I want to feel your presence, Lord. Father, set me on fire, Father. Just give me grace, Lord, and Lord, please bless me, Lord."

Seriously? Would you talk to your boss at work like that? Would your best friend continue to be your best friend if you talked like that to him or her? That's how we talk to someone we *don't* know and don't trust. Think about that.

Do any of your prayers sound the same, time after time? When you pray, does God say, "Here comes the same ole, same ole recording again… ." If you pray like that, you run the risk of God just tuning you out … just as your best friend would if you sounded like that.

Endeavor to be like Enoch. We learn about him from Genesis 5:24 and Hebrews 11:5. God enjoyed Enoch's prayers by faith (talking to God whom he couldn't see, but he did so as if he could) so much, that God must have said something like, "I enjoy your prayers so much, I want to enjoy your company face to face. Why don't you just come up here and hang out with me?" And he did! The Bible says he was not found, which means people looked and looked for him. His prayers were so good, he bypassed death!

In Mark 14:36, when Jesus prayed, He addressed God as "Abba Father," which to us is like saying "Daddy." That has a bit of reverence but a whole lot of endearing connections of love, trust, openness, and closeness. It involves a hug.

But that was Jesus. Can *we* address God as "Abba Father"? Romans 8:16 says yes we can! This same verse adds that the Holy Spirit is there with us, sort of like showing up with His arm around us in a show of support. The passage also says God considers us His children and joint heirs with Jesus. Wow, that's wonderfully heartwarming, and therefore we are welcome in the presence of God just like Jesus is, and you can talk freely as you are.

"WHAT DOES PRAYING DO; SHOULD I EVEN BOTHER?"

Prayer is a way of humbling ourselves before God. James 4:10 says, "Humble yourselves in the sight of the Lord, and He will lift you up." Being humble is required to glorify God. Remember the parable in Luke 18:9–14 about the Pharisee and the tax collector that came to pray? The tax collector was humbled and asked for God's mercy. And according to the passage, God heard his prayer, and the man was justified.

Prayer is a way of slowing us down and allowing us to concentrate on what matters most. In our world of fast-paced, instant gratification and the need to do something important or gratifying constantly, prayer is something God wants us to do to get away from all that for a period of time. Prayer is not a waste of time, nor is it a futile ritual for the weak or needy; it is the most important use of time in your whole day and the most powerful and productive thing you can do. James 5:16–18 is a very real promise ("The effective, fervent prayer of a righteous man avails much" is part of that passage). You will understand that by the end of this chapter and when you see God, honor this promise.

God wants us to have faith that He will hear our prayers. Jesus said in Matthew 21:22, "Whatever things you ask in prayer, believing, you will receive." The word "believing" means having faith. God always answers prayers. His answer may be "Yes," or it may be "No, because I have a better answer," or even "Not now; it's best for you to wait." Have faith God knows what's best for you and *does* answer.

Jesus removed the sin barrier preventing our communication with God; however, sin has a way of keeping us from praying. I'm sure you know what I'm saying. Perhaps you stumbled and did something you shouldn't, and you now feel guilty and bad about it. You now *don't* pray because you think God is upset or disappointed in you and won't hear your prayers. Wrong! That's when you *should* pray. Thanks to Jesus, God doesn't see your sin. If you are a true Christian, He sees you the same way He sees Jesus! Sin prevents you from experiencing the joys, forgiveness, and blessing of praying.

To paraphrase a famous John Bunyan quote: Prayer will drive out the sin from your life, or sin will drive out the prayer from your life.

Life is better when you communicate regularly with God, and it frankly sucks when you don't. A good indication of how close you are to God is how often you talk to Him and how often you praise Him and thank Him for things throughout your day.

"MY PRAYERS ARE LAME; I NEED SOME HELP."

You have help! The Holy Spirit will help us pray. Romans 8:26 says, "Likewise the Spirit also helps us in our weaknesses. For we do not know what we should pray for as we ought, but the Spirit himself makes intercession for us with groaning which cannot be uttered."

God also wants us to know that because of Jesus, we can come confidently and boldly before Him. Hebrews 4:14–16 tells us Jesus is our advocate in heaven, and because of Him we can come boldly to God's throne and obtain mercy and grace.

Growing up in Wyoming, I was involved in 4-H. It's basically Scouts for farm kids, where you pick a few projects and work on them, then get judged and win awards if you did well. I remember thinking the wonderful life skills 4-H taught me should be open to more kids my age who were not necessarily from agriculture-based families. I wanted to add projects city kids could do. I also wanted projects with little expense so kids from poor or single-parent families could participate.

Basic electricity was one of those ideas, where a young person could learn how electricity works, some basic safety precautions, how to repair a broken plug on the end of a chord, or make an extension cord from broken small appliances. Another was model rocketry, which has since become one of the more popular 4-H projects!

So, at fifteen years of age, I put together my ideas and sought to get them to the national head of 4-H, which happened to be the US secretary of agriculture in Washington, DC. How is a Wyoming farm kid going to talk to the secretary of agriculture? Well, my dad went to college with our Wyoming senator, who was in Washington, so I wrote a letter to him about my ideas and wishes for 4-H.

Amazingly enough, that senator liked my letter, and I flew to Washington, DC, where he took me to Capitol Hill right into the office of the US secretary of agriculture. I wore the suit my parents bought me for my high school prom, which I still didn't actually fit into yet ... a tan suit with dark brown patches on the sleeves (which were too long), with my tie hanging down below my zipper. Just before we entered the office, the wise senator asked me who my favorite teacher was. Though it seemed like a strange question, I told him. He then told me not to be scared or nervous when I met the secretary, but to talk to him just as I would with that school teacher I liked and respected.

We went into the secretary's office together, his hand behind my right shoulder so I could feel his encouraging support, which calmed me a little and gave me confidence. Our senator greeted the secretary of agriculture, exchanged a few pleasantries and, as he squeezed my shoulder, quickly said, "Mr. Secretary, spend a few minutes listening to what this young man has to say. It's important to him, and I would suggest honoring his requests." Wow! That was impressive! I felt so important!

I remembered the senator's advice about my favorite teacher, so with butterflies in my stomach and cold, shaky hands (which I curled up hidden in the too-long sleeves of my suit jacket), I just opened my mouth, thanked the secretary for his time, and started telling him what was on my mind about 4-H projects for city and underprivileged kids. I told him why they were needed, what my suggestions were, and respectfully asked for his help to make them happen. He did, and the results are those two projects previously mentioned, and others too!

Jesus is sort of like that senator. He can get us right into the throne room of the universe and say to the almighty God, "Spend some time listening to what this person has to say, and I suggest an appropriate answer." As Hebrews 4:16 says, because of Jesus and His advice, we can talk boldly before our Father God.

Hebrews 7:25 and Romans 8:24 tell us Jesus lives right now and makes intercessions for us in heaven. He prays for us, probably communicating more effectively with God our Father than we ever could. That's *so* comforting! It's very impressive and makes us important to God.

"So, How Do I Pray ... and What for?"

Praying to God it is just like talking with that secretary of agriculture: Talk normally, with a little structure and a *lot* of purpose—oh, and maybe as if talking to your favorite teacher if it helps you. Jesus gave advice on what we should say, and He even provided His disciples a pattern to follow in Matthew 6:9–13. Most people call it the Lord's Prayer, but it is actually a pattern Jesus taught His disciples to follow because they hadn't prayed before. We can use this same advice and pattern. Jesus didn't mean you and I have to repeat it; in fact, just a couple verses prior, Jesus said to not use vain repetitions. He meant for us to follow the guidelines He suggested, which is why Jesus starts off with, "In this manner ...," which means follow this style or form. Here is the prayer and some suggested wording you might pray as an example:

"In this manner, therefore, pray:
Our Father in heaven, Hallowed be Your name."

You: "Dear Heavenly Father, you alone are awesome! Being able to talk to you and know you listen to me brings me to my knees before you in awe!"

"Your kingdom come."

You: "Your kingdom involves love, joy, peace, truth, beauty, compassion, trust, grace, and selflessness. I want those to be part of my life when I interact with others today and every day until Jesus comes. Please help me to have those in my life, and bring a sample of your kingdom to others around me."

"Your will be done. On earth as it is in heaven."

You: "I ask that you orchestrate and control everything in my life today, just as if I was with you in heaven, and that you work out every difficult situation or occurrence for my good and your glory."

"Give us this day our daily bread."

You: "Please provide for my basic needs. You know what I need today; please take care of those for me. You also know I need _____, and would you please _____? Can you please help my friend _____ today? He is struggling with _____. Please give him wisdom and help him to be gracious. Also, you know Mrs. _____ who lost her husband recently; please comfort her and take care of all her needs.

"And forgive us our debts, as we forgive our debtors."

You: "Please forgive me when I sinned or messed up doing _____ and _____. And, when others I deal with today sin or do something against me, I will forgive them as you did. Please help me to do that, and remind me if I forget."

"And do not lead us into temptation,"

You: "You know how I struggle with _____. Please don't allow that temptation or any others to hit me today, but if they do, please give me strength and a focus on You to help me to overcome it before I stumble."

"But deliver us from the evil one."

You: "Keep Satan or any of his cronies away from me. Please put a hedge of protection around me. If any of his attempts get through, please give me wisdom and strength to resist them so they flee. Please remind me you are more powerful than them and that your spirit should guide me, not my worldly lusts or desires."

"For Yours is the kingdom and the power
and the glory forever. Amen."

You: "Please help me to enhance your kingdom today, to serve you, to rely on your power instead of mine, and to do everything today in such a way that it brings glory to *you*, in ways that continue and multiply! In the wonderful name and assumed agreement of Jesus, I pray this prayer, amen."

You will notice one very important theme in the Lord's Prayer: "Me" or "I" are not in there, but "our," "we," and "us" sure are. We can certainly pray for ourselves, but the majority of our prayers that glorify God are centered on others.

A suggestion for praying is to read Psalm 91 and pray for what's in there. Notice verses 3–8 are about God's care, 9–13 are about your guardian angel, and 14–16 are God's speaking about you.

Here are some useful prayer tips and strategies:

- Pray from your fingers.
  - Index finger: Pray for teachers and/or your pastor
  - Middle: Government or employment leaders
  - Ring: Spouse and/or those who are weak or hurt
  - Pinky: Yourself.
  - Thumb: Family or others you know
- Start a prayer journal. Write down what you are going to say and work your way through it, including what was answered and how. (It's okay to open your eyes and read from your notes during prayer.)
- Create a "war room." A place with notes and mementos to help you pray and remember who to pray for.

These are just a few examples. What's important is to use what works for *you*. But, remember, God likes to hear from you like a loving father loves to hear from his kids. I never asked my dad for a quick chat, then took him right to my closet where I had sticky notes, an acorn from the missionary I met at church, and a photo of my grandmother who is ill. You don't have to be ritualistic about praying, and there is no formula or posturing needed to cause Him to hear you. It's all about communicating respectfully with your loving Father in heaven and developing your relationship with Him.

Don't worry if you mess up or didn't pray very well. He just loves to hear from you! In fact, remember this: Jesus is at this very moment now sitting at the right hand of God, interceding for you. He is *your* advocate in front of God. Remember, Jesus loves you so much He died for you, and He wants what's the very best for you, so He talks to God for you so those good things happen. He fills in the blanks with words you can't remember. He explains to God the Father what you were asking for, but He does so a whole lot more effectively than you. If that doesn't light your fire and make you warm all over, your wood is wet …

One of the bonuses of prayer is connecting with others. *What?* Yep. When you hear of someone's struggles, do you ever say, "I will pray for you"? You should because it's a wonderful thing to say. Other people always appreciate that, but do you really pray for them? Or was that a figure of speech like "let's do lunch" … a nice thing to say, but something you don't really intend to do …

Praying for others is called intercessory prayer. This is where you can—and should— intercede on behalf of others as you kneel before the creator and sustainer of everything. It really is something wonderful and generous you can do for them (and you). Remember, God loves relationships. He loves people. He brought people into existence, and He just *loves* it when we care for other people enough to pray for them. I think He also loves to answer those prayers, just to keep the relationship thing going strong. If you pray for others and they pray for you, that circle is exactly as God intends, with Him keeping the circle going. Give it a try! You will be amazed, and you will be blessed.

Talking to men about God is a great thing, but talking to God about men is greater still.
—E. M. Bounds

"BUT DOES GOD EVEN HEAR ME?"

Do you ever think, "I doubt God hears my prayers; He sure doesn't seem to answer them." Since I firmly believe God hears and answers every prayer of mine, and I have countless specific examples of His answers, I often wonder why some Christians may think that … or why God actually doesn't answer their prayers. I know some of you honestly don't get answers, and I sympathize with you and may be able to help. Here are some possibilities for you to consider and what the Bible (especially Jesus) says about each one:

You don't specifically ask.

So I say to you, ask, and it will be given to you; seek, and you will find; knock, and it will be opened to you. For everyone who asks receives, and he who seeks finds, and to him who knocks it will be opened. If a son asks for bread from any father among you, will he give him a stone? Or if he asks for a fish, will he give him a serpent instead of a fish? Or if he asks for an egg, will he offer him a scorpion? If you then, being evil, know how to give good gifts to your children, how much more will your heavenly Father give the Holy Spirit to those who ask Him! (Luke 11:9–13)

"If you abide in Me, and My words abide in you, you will ask what you desire, and it shall be done for you" (John 15:7).

"And whatever you ask in My name, that I will do, that the Father may be glorified in the Son. If you ask anything in My name, I will do it" (John 14:13–14).

You doubt.

"But let him ask in faith, with no doubting, for he who doubts is like a wave of the sea driven and tossed by the wind. For let not that man suppose that he will receive anything from the Lord; he is a double-minded man, unstable in all his ways" (James 1:6–8).

You ask wrongly … and for stupid stuff.

"You ask and do not receive, because you ask amiss [wrongly], that you may spend it on your pleasures" (James 4:3). By the way, the original Greek word for "amiss" is *kak-oce',* from which we get the word caca … yep, your prayers are crappy.

You aren't "abiding" in Christ.

"If you abide in Me, and My words abide in you, you will ask what you desire, and it shall be done for you" (John 15:7).

You don't have faith God will answer

"And whatever things you ask in prayer, believing, you will receive" (Matt. 21:22).

You pray to be or look "religious."

And when you pray, you shall not be like the hypocrites. For they love to pray standing in the synagogues and on the corners of the streets, that they may be seen by men. Assuredly, I say to you, they have their reward. But you, when you pray, go into your room, and when you have shut your door, pray to your Father who is in the secret place; and your Father who sees in secret will reward you openly. (Matt. 6:5–6)

You pray selfishly, as if you know better than God.

"Not my will, but yours be done" (Luke 22:42).

You turned away from God, or don't read the Bible anymore.

"One who turns away his ear from hearing the law, Even his prayer is an abomination" (Prov. 28:9).

You value a sin in your life more than God.

"If I regard iniquity in my heart, the Lord will not hear" (Ps. 66:18).

"Now we know that God does not hear sinners; but if anyone is a worshipper of God and does His will, He hears him" (John 9:31).

You have idols where God should be.

God says, "Son of man, these men have taken their idols into their hearts, and set the stumbling block of their iniquity before their faces. Should I indeed let myself be consulted by them?" (Ezek. 14:3 ESV).

Your prayers don't line up with God's will.

"Now this is the confidence that we have in Him, that if we ask anything according to His will, He hears us" (1 John 5:14).

You treat your spouse wrongly.

"Husbands, likewise, dwell with them with understanding, giving honor to the wife, as to the weaker vessel, and as being heirs together of the grace of life, that your prayers may not be hindered" (1 Pet. 3:7).

"HOW DO I KNOW GOD WILL ANSWER?"

Maybe it will help if you fully understand this promise from the first mega church pastor (the church in Jerusalem)—His name was James, and he wrote in a book something he saw actually occur among the people in his church: "The effective, fervent prayer of a righteous person avails much" (James 5:16). You see, God works with righteous people to accomplish common wishes and goals. Are you righteous? Do you have wishes? You are righteous in the eyes of God if you have accepted Jesus as your Savior. That means God will hear you and will answer!

I believe God answers all of our prayers when they line up with His will. That may be an intangible comment, but this may help: Is what you are praying for something Jesus would also want for you? That is actually why we end our prayers with "in Jesus' name, amen."

In John 14:13–14 Jesus said, "And whatever you ask in My name, that I will do, that the Father may be glorified in the Son. If you ask anything in My name, I will do it." Doesn't that give you confidence about your prayers!? Even though ending our prayers with the statement "in Jesus' name" isn't in itself an "abracadabra" statement that makes your prayers happen, it's simply a way of saying "I think what I prayed for is something Jesus would agree with." You don't have to end your prayers with it; it's more of a reminder for you than for God.

"And this is the confidence that we have toward him, that if we ask anything according to his will he hears us. And if we know that he hears us in whatever we ask, we know that we have the requests that we have asked of him" 1 John 5:14–15 (ESV).

Usually, God answers our prayers with any of these responses: "Yes," "no," "later," or "I have something better for you." Remember, God loves you like a wise and generous daddy. Galatians 4:6–7 reminds us of that, and He loves to do things for you that you will thank or praise Him for. So rest assured, praying avails much!

Oh, one other thing? The term "amen" means "so be it." It's like signing your name at the end of a letter.

PRAYERS ARE ANSWERED WHEN YOU AND GOD ARE ON THE SAME PAGE.

Let's face it: we are greedy and selfish. Really. We want things, we want them now, and we get upset when we don't get them. We complain and whine and cry and pout. We are scared and worried and needy. Then, when we pray, we express all of those traits but try really hard to sound mature and spiritual. God probably smiles or laughs, giving Jesus a little wink, but the good thing is God knows that's how most of us are and loves us anyway … as He listens to us anyway.

We do, however, need to realize God's love, as well as His character and even His righteous agenda, as best we can. That helps us not be so childish and needy, enabling us to line up better with whom we have been created in the image of. Here are some suggestions to help your "page of prayer requests" become closer to God's or, actually, be on the "same page as God's":

- Your page says, "Please give me an easy day." God's page says, "I will give you strength with My own power."
- Your page says, "Please let me win the lottery." God's page says, "Seek first My kingdom, and all these things will be added to you."
- Your page says, "Please help me pass this test I didn't study for." God's page says, "The diligent and hardworking are rewarded."
- Your page says, "Why am I sick; why won't you heal me?" God's page says, "My grace is sufficient for you; the sooner you learn that, the better you will be."
- Your page says, "I am so tired of this time of trouble; I have no idea why it's happening to me." God's page says, "I am allowing this so you can be stronger and be more like Jesus, and when this season of trouble ends for you, you can help others going through it."
- Your page says, "Please don't have her call me; I don't want to go help her." God's page says, "Don't grow weary of doing good; you will get rewarded in due season."
- Your page says, "Please get me out of this." God's page says, "I want you to go through that so you will learn patience and be able to help others go through that too."
- Your page says, "I don't want to go to church today." God's page says, "I have a special blessing for you today you won't want to miss."
- Your page says, "Please don't have him come over here. I don't know what to say." God's page says, "I will give you some things to say to that guy—things I want him to hear that will change his life for the better."

PRAYER, TRUSTING GOD, AND AN ENGINE

Prayer involves *trust*: trusting God with the competent and correct answer. Prayer to God and not trusting Him with the results is like putting gasoline in a car that is missing the engine. You certainly could do that, but it would be a waste! Yet so many of us ask God for things in prayer and have little or no confidence in Him answering those requests. That may be because His answers are sometimes different than we want or slower than we hope. He is a lot smarter and more powerful than we are, and He can see into our future. We just need to understand He will *always* answer … in ways better than we actually want.

Think about that car/engine analogy a little further. The car's engine has three basic components: the block, the ignition (spark plugs, power coil, fuel injectors), and the pistons (connected to the crank and wheels). All three of them work together to power the car down the road. Let me explain this analogy further:

Engine block. This all-encompassing case of the engine is the part of prayer I call "thankfulness." Trusting God comes from remembering how He answered past prayers and then entrusting Him with new ones. Thanking Him tells you (and Him) something wonderful happened, something attributable only to Him.

Ignition. God is powerful (power coil), He is in charge (spark plugs), and He loves you (as in fuel that's ignited by the other two).

Pistons and crank. These do the work. Jesus did the work on the cross so you can talk to God, and the Holy Spirit helps accomplish God's will. They work with the previous two and move you down the road of life.

All you have to do is put gasoline in the car (prayer) and enjoy the ride. That's a great one-liner to remember. But here are a few more:

- The key to your successful prayer life is trusting God with the answers.
- Do your absolute best and give God the rest.

Is prayer your steering wheel or your spare tire?
—Corrie ten Boom

Prayer can never be in excess.
—Charles Spurgeon

To be a Christian without prayer is no more possible than to be alive without breathing.
—Martin Luther

Prayer gets us on God's agenda, not God on our agenda.
—Dr. James MacDonald

We look upon prayer as a means of getting things for ourselves; the Bible's idea of prayer is that we may get to know God himself.
—Oswald Chambers

The prayer offered to God in the morning during your quiet time is the key that unlocks the door of the day. Any athlete knows that it is the start that ensures a good finish.
—Adrian Rogers

In 2008, when the great recession came, my steel fabrication business really suffered. Some customers stopped paying their invoices or found "excuses" to not pay, and new work became elusive. I'm sure you've heard similar stories. I always knew I needed God's help daily and prayed a lot for His help, but one day in 2009 I made the commitment to get out of bed half an hour earlier each day, go to a quiet place downstairs, get on my knees and pray "fervently."

Those daily times in prayer changed my life! God became more real to me than in all my previous forty years of walking with Him. God honored my prayers. God proved to me *He is real, loves me, and loves to answer my prayers.*

I still cherish that prayer time each day. You should too. It's the foundation of a good day. It brings glory to Him.

PRACTICAL APPLICATIONS

1. Set a specific time each day for personal alone time talking with God.

2. _____

   _____

3. _____

   _____

2 FAITH (AND HOPE)

Faith is the substance of things hoped for, the evidence of things not seen (Heb. 11:1). Then, in Hebrews 11:6, we learn that without faith it is impossible to please God, so to glorify God, you must first believe that He *is* and that He is a rewarder of those who diligently (faithfully) seek Him.

Faith, as you just read, is extremely important to God. Faith defines us as Christians, even to the extent that those who are not believers call us "a person of faith."

"WHAT IS FAITH, REALLY? I DON'T THINK I KNOW ENOUGH TO HAVE FAITH."

The number-one issue in the New Testament is faith in Jesus. Jesus is the only pathway to salvation or being right with God. Faith in Jesus rejects all other ways of salvation, and there is no need to add anything else to Jesus, "There is no other name under heaven given among men by which we must be saved." (Acts 4:12) To have faith in Jesus means to believe Jesus is the Son of God, came and died and rose again, and you trust Him both simply, and completely.

Let's delve into what faith is a little more deeply. I believe God gives us about 75 percent of what we need to know to believe in Him. Think about that for a minute. When you first became a Christian, did you know *everything* about God? Did you fully comprehend Jesus? Romans 1:20, Psalm 19:1–4, and Psalm 148:1–10 say the creation gives us evidence there is a God, enough evidence to draw a conclusion there is a God. The earth and the heavens are sort of a missionary. But everything isn't explained … you still have to kick in just a little to round out the evidence … and that what we kick in is called faith.

Here is a fun one: Think about this one when hiking in the mountains or watching *The Sound of Music*: "You will go out in joy and be led forth in peace; the mountains and hills will burst into song before you, and all the trees of the field will clap their hands" (Isa. 55:12).

God dwells in His creation and is everywhere indivisibly present in all His works. He is transcendent above all His works even while He is immanent within them.
—A.W. Tozer

But that only gives us a little bit of knowledge of God, probably not enough to know we are sinners and need to repent of our sins and accept Jesus as our Lord and Savior. Each of us had some knowledge of God when we were saved, but not full knowledge. Some other things have been said to us, or we have read in the Bible, and may understand a little, but not all.

When we can take that incomplete set of "facts" and say to God, "I don't fully know everything about you or what you say, but I am going to take what I *do* know and go with that." When we believe based on that limited amount, I think that pleases God, and He takes our less than full percentage, say 75 percent, and considers it as if a full 100 percent. If fact, true faith then doesn't even dwell on the missing 25 percent. What's "missing" doesn't bother us. And sometimes God fills in a good amount of that remaining 25 percent. So that is my definition of faith: Believing God even when we don't have all the facts, and what's missing doesn't matter to us.

I've heard this acronym of faith: *Full Assurance In The Heart.* Even though we may not know everything, we know enough and call that good. Full assurance in our heart that God is who He says He is and full assurance in our heart we can trust Him … in everything … thus, "full assurance." Do you have full assurance or full trust in God? You glorify Him when you do.

In John 4:46–54, Jesus was in Cana, and a man whose son was sick back at his house in Capernaum walked about twenty miles uphill to ask Jesus to heal his son. Jesus healed his son right from there in Cana and told the man, "Go your way; your son lives." The man believed the word that Jesus spoke and headed down the hill back home. His son did get healed, and it was because the man believed Jesus' words right there at the time he heard them … not after he saw his son well. Faith is believing God's words then and there, not waiting for proof or confirmation or "signs and wonders."

Faith is believing in God (John 14:1), Jesus (John 6:29; Acts 20:21), the good news of the gospel (Mark 1:15), and God's promises (Rom. 4:21; Heb. 11:13).

Faith gets you freedom from the penalty of your sins (Rom. 3:21–22, 28, 30; Acts 16:31), eternal life (John 3:15–16), access to God (Rom. 5:2; Eph. 3:12), moral and intellectual improvement (1 Tim. 1:4; Jude 20), God's promises (Gal. 3:22; Heb. 6:12), an adopted child of God (Gal. 3:26), and the assistance of the Helper or the Holy Spirit (Gal. 3:14; Acts 11:15–17)

No wonder having faith pleases God … it pleases God to give you all that cool stuff!!

"I JUST DON'T SEEM TO HAVE MUCH FAITH."

When you fall asleep, you have faith you will wake up. You even have faith you will wake up in the same place. When you sit in a chair, you have faith it will hold you up. When you fly in an airplane, you have faith the air you cannot see will hold up the plane all the way until your destination. And you have faith in the pilot to get you there too. Spiritual things are really not different at all. But some seem to have more than others, just like some people are very fearful of flying, and some are not.

Faith is something you are given a measure of. Some people have more faith than others. But we all should have some and are expected to use and demonstrate it. We can see that in Romans 12:3–8 where Paul said, "God has dealt to each one a measure of faith." Later in the passage, he said that God gives us gifts by His grace "in proportion to our faith."

1 Corinthians 12:9 indicates faith is a spiritual gift, so those who have a lot should help those who have little. Also, you are to have faith to be able to use the gifts you have. Faith is needed to function and serve as a Christian.

In Matthew 17:20 Jesus said, "[I]f you have faith as a mustard seed, you will say to this mountain, 'Move from here to there,' and it will move; and nothing will be impossible for you."

Jesus implied faith can do wonderful things, but those things are neither because of you nor from you. They're from only God. The source and the object of faith is the one and only awesome and powerful God. Jesus, who does not exaggerate or even fib a little, sure gave a good description of the power of faith, didn't He?! That alone should help you have more faith.

Now, these previous passages are saying one very important thing. The measure of faith we have is by the grace of God. So no one can boast or be "thinking of themselves more highly than they ought to think" (Rom. 12:3). In the passages cited earlier, Paul says that not only do your spiritual gifts come from the grace of God but also the faith to carry them out. So that eliminates any pride. Guess what: putting into practice your spiritual gift(s) without pride glorifies God!

"CAN I GET MORE FAITH?"

Can you increase the amount of faith you presently have? Yes. Romans 10:17 says, "So then faith comes by hearing, and hearing by the word of God." You can gain more faith by reading the Bible and listening to biblical sermons. In John 15:7, Jesus says, "If you abide in Me, and My words abide in you, you will ask what you desire, and it shall be done for you." Reading and believing what God says in His Word builds faith, especially when you read of others who exercised faith.

In addition, Jesus also says that when His words in the Bible are part of your life, you will have the faith that all your requests will be granted. When you see that happen, your faith will increase. Increasing your faith is tied to the practical application of Jesus' words into your life.

Faith is something you are tested on. James 1:2–3 says when trials come, you are to "count it all joy," because your faith is being tested. You will learn things about yourself then. You will also learn about your relationship with God. You have the opportunity to show God your faith.

In so doing, James says, you will learn patience … something we all have to learn, because patience doesn't come naturally. Patience is a product of faith. And you can get more of each!

Faith is something that keeps you with God and His purposes for your life, and the lack of faith can destroy your relationship and usefulness to God. During the Last Supper, Jesus knew Peter would deny Him three times later that night. Jesus alludes to this soon-to-occur event to Peter, knowing that his denying Jesus could devastate Peter's relationship and usefulness to Jesus, from which he might not recover. (You can read this in Luke 22:31–32.) Sticking up for your relationship with Jesus builds more faith.

Now, let's be honest: I probably would have done the same thing as Peter, and I also think we all can relate to Peter in many ways. However, knowing this about Peter, and ourselves, will help us not faithlessly deny Jesus, much like seeing someone else burn their hand on a stove will help us decide to not put our hand there either.

Also, notice Jesus didn't prevent Peter from denying Him those three times. When Peter realized his error, it was only through the relentless love and forgiveness of Jesus that Peter learned to have more faith! John 21:15–17 tells of Jesus restoring Peter, and one example of the result is Peter's fantastic sermon beginning in Acts 2:14

Faith is something you need encouragement from others to improve, and you should encourage others as well. Paul realized this right away in his magnificent letter to the Romans in chapter 1:11–12: "For I long to see you, that I may impart to you some spiritual gift, so that you may be established— that is, that I may be encouraged together with you by the mutual faith both of you and me."

Faith is what Jesus prayed that Peter would maintain … and it would get him through some very tough times, times that Satan would use to drag Peter away from the Lord Jesus. Jesus loved Peter's zeal but realized his faith was weak (again, most of us can relate to Peter). He didn't tell Peter to always love Him or pay attention to what he thought or said so he won't stumble; no, Jesus went to the root of Peter's (and our) relationship and usefulness. He said to Peter "Indeed, Satan has asked for you, that he may sift you as wheat. But I have prayed for you, that your faith should not fail."

Faith is what keeps you strong during the tough times in your life too … when Satan wants to tear you down and destroy your relationship with Jesus. When your faith fails, you are doomed. Remember Peter walked on water when his eyes were fixed on Jesus, but when he took his eyes off Jesus and looked at the rough waves around him, he sank. Maintaining faith through the hard times in your life, as well as the good, takes effort and focus on Jesus, and when you give effort to keep it, you gain more and more faith … and God is glorified.

Do you know someone whose faith is being tested or is slipping? Consider encouraging them … which glorifies God. They may resist you, but at least try. Learn to "listen" to the Holy Spirit in you when He prompts you to go sit with them a bit. Help them with their faith.

"SOUNDS GREAT, BUT CAN MY FAITH GET STRONGER AND MORE ENDURING?"

The apostle Paul told the people in the Thessaloniki church in 2 Thessalonians 1:3 that their faith was growing exceedingly. So it is possible for your faith to increase and get stronger. In fact, Acts 16:3 tells us just that: Our faith can get stronger and stronger.

Faith is something you must practice and demonstrate to prove you have it, and doing so actually helps grow your faith's endurance, just like working out at a gym. James 2:20 tells us faith without works is dead. So make an effort to demonstrate your faith, as doing so will help you have more. Do some "good works" where you serve others. Help a widow clean her house or volunteer to help at vacation Bible school or visit someone sick or hurting. Teach a Sunday school class or lead a small group Bible study one or more times.

In Acts 14:9 Paul saw a crippled man, "observing him intently and seeing that he had faith to be healed… ." Faith can be something others see in you. Endeavor to have faith others notice.

One of the main ways you demonstrate and grow your faith is to *serve* Him. Another way to grow your faith is to let others help *you*. Attend a small group Bible study or accountability group. Paul realized this right away in his magnificent letter to the Romans 1:11–12: For I long to see you, that I may impart to you some spiritual gift, so that you may be established—that is, that I may be encouraged together with you by the mutual faith both of you and me."

Paul expanded on this by using the analogy of a "shield of faith" in his teaching on the armor of God in Ephesians 6. The Roman soldiers used their shields together for strength in defense and offense when in battle: the soldier would hold on to his shield with one hand and grab the shield of the soldier next to him to form strong protection when the whole platoon did this together.

"CAN I LOSE SOME OF MY FAITH?"

It's a bummer, but yes, you can. Paul tells us we can lose some of our faith in 1 Timothy 1:3–6 where he says to not give heed to false doctrines, fables, idle talk, and endless genealogies that cause disputes rather than godly edification (remember, godly edification produces faith). Discussions that have no logical end or that stray from God's truth can result in you losing faith.

I think this occurs by the design of Satan, to cause us to have doubts. Doubt is the main tool Satan uses to get us away from God and lose faith. In fact, doubt is like a cancer: If we allow it to continue, it can wreak havoc in our spiritual lives and cause other sickly things in our lives too. Doubt is the soil from which fear, worry, and anxiety grow. Those things all cause us to focus on ourselves, not on God in faith.

Maybe you have non-Christian friends or relatives whose argumentative talk comes from false humanistic or new-age ideas, and it's wearing you down. Or maybe you are in a tough spot in life or some sad events have occurred where doubts are creeping in and you are questioning your faith. Conversations with coworkers that have no usefulness is another way to get your faith down. Such "Debbie Downer" conversations about politics or politicians, "what-if" scenarios, and doomsday scenarios sure can wear you—and your faith—down. Paul says don't hang around too long when this occurs, and certainly don't give heed to them (as in don't let them have any effect on you).

Here is a practical and useful suggestion for allowing God to stabilize your faith when it's sliding downhill. This is guaranteed to stop your sliding or deteriorating faith, stabilize and encourage you that you *do* have faith, and even increase your faith: Psalm 37:3 says to "feed on His faithfulness."

Recall the times in your life when God's truth was clearly evident to you or was faithful to you ... remember specific events where He answered your prayers or brought you through a tough time. Deposit those in your memory bank and withdraw them as needed. The word "feed" in that passage means draw nourishment from ... to gain strength from God's faithfulness. Use your "positive bank balance" to strengthen your faith in Him.

God is the same yesterday, as today, as He will be tomorrow. So how faithful He was to you in the past is how He will be today and tomorrow. Your faith only increases when you learn to trust God, which comes from recalling His goodness. Faith believes and relies upon God's good character and His promises and His power.

The opposite of faith is doubt. Now, I say opposite, but you cannot doubt if you don't have *some* faith. However, if you let doubts overshadow what God says in His Word, it's like giving Satan your hand: He will then gleefully pull you down and away from God. Satan *wants* you to doubt. It's his best tactic to get Christians away from living a life of joy and glorifying God. After all, Satan wants nothing more than for you to have a life of worry, fear, depression ... and be a useless Christian. Remember, doubt is the soil that only weeds grow out of: weeds of apathy, fear, anxieties, self-centeredness, worry, sinful behavior and, sometimes, even depression. Clean that dirt of doubt out of your life, and you will not lose any faith.

FAITH PRODUCES HOPE

Faith and hope go hand in hand. Faith sees opportunities and brighter tomorrows. This produces hope. Godly hope does not disappoint ... so if your hope disappoints you, your hope is in the wrong place. God will cause all things to work together for your good if you love Him and are living according to His purposes (Rom. 8:28), and God will complete the good He has started in you (Phil. 1:6).

- Faith is an intentional attitude.
- Faith looks for ways; doubt looks for obstacles.

- Faith sees your proper place and perspective. That usually that means we are small and limited, and God is big and powerful.
- Faith says it's okay to have faith … which is not needing to know everything. Faith is understanding you are not smarter than God.
- Faith trusts and allows God.
- Faith grows the roots of hope.

Hope is the confident expectation that what God says is true and will happen and will eventually be wonderful for you. It doesn't disappoint, because of God's love and the Helper (the Holy Spirit) who is in you. Their knowledge of you and what's best for you are what you trust in … and trust is an offshoot of faith. (You may want to read those two sentences again.)

Hope that is desirably lofty and great should be based on a system or live person who is capable of making your hope happen, not based on things or riches than may not or on dead people who cannot. That capable person is Jesus. What you hope for is determined by whom you live for. If hope disappoints, then it was a false hope, or it was based on an incapable person or system. Jesus never disappoints, He loves you beyond what you can imagine, and He is alive right now, sitting right next to God the Father, the creator and sustainer of all that is.

When you place your hope in Jesus and His system called the gospel, you can rest assured your hope is forever intact and will never disappoint. It may be delayed a bit when it doesn't match your time frame, but it always comes true, exceeding your expectations. First Peter 1:21 says faith and hope are in God, who raised Jesus from the dead, an event no one disputes and we even have a holiday for.

Faith and hope together are what keep you going in difficult times if you are diligent to keep a focus on them and what or whom they point to. We are encouraged to keep focusing on God's promises of a full abundant life (John 10:10) and eternal life (John 3:16) with Him, even to the end of our days. Hebrews 6:11 says, "And we desire that each one of you show the same diligence to the full assurance of hope until the end, that you do not become sluggish, but imitate those who through faith and patience inherit the promises."

When faith and hope come together, they result in *courage*. Courage is that *gumption* it takes to buck up and do something uncomfortable, possibly painful, or downright scary. John Wayne famously said, "Courage is being scared to death, and saddling up anyway."[2]

I like to say, do your best and give God the rest. That leads us to another essential element of glorifying God … and an essential element of a worthwhile Christian life: Trusting God.

FAITH PRODUCES TRUST

Trust is like the blue jeans you put on your faith. Trust is the act that shows God (and others) the faith you have. Hopefully, you show your trust by trusting God with all your heart (Prov. 3:5), by giving your cares to Him, for He cares for you, and knowing He will take care of them in a way that is best for you (1 Pet. 5:7).

You also glorify God when you trust Him by doing your best, working with your best effort, and understanding God will supply all your needs as Philippians 4:19 says, "And my God shall supply all your need according to His riches in glory by Christ Jesus." We're also reminded, in verse eleven, you glorify Him by being content: "Not that I speak in regard to need, for I have learned in whatever state I am, to be content." Notice Paul said he had to *learn* to be content, because contentment doesn't come naturally, but when you focus on God's faithfulness, trustworthiness, sovereignty, and lovingkindness, you become content, and the spiritual maturity of that is glorifying to Him. Glorifying God by trusting Him is especially true during trials, as James 1 tells us, for they are tests of our faith, and we glorify Him when we go through trials with full faith and trust in Him. God also loves it when we are dependent on Him, and that brings glory to Him, not to ourselves or what we have attained.

"The only way to learn strong faith is to endure great trials," Charles Mueller said.[3] Because when you go through trials and come out the other side seeing how faithful God was to you, your trust in Him is strengthened.

Trust gives us confidence, like an Olympic athlete who trusts he or she will win their race. That's what Paul said in 2 Corinthians 3:4–5: We have such trust through Christ toward God, because we have all sufficiency [abilities, help, and favorable outcome] from God.

What do you think of when you hear the word "trust"? It's a word that connotes immense value, doesn't it?! Trust is something you value, and it makes you valuable to God … an interesting concept, isn't it?! Yet, the Scriptures are full of examples of God using people who trusted Him, and the reverse is also readily apparent.

Trust is a wonderful thing to both you and the trustee (the person being trusted). It is said that a godly marriage is built on trust, and without trust, the relationship crumbles. A glorious marriage has both spouses trusting each other. Do you see then, how your relationship with God, if you trust Him, brings glory to Him and your relationship with Him?

Proverbs 3:5–6 involves just this kind of trust: "Trust in the LORD with all your heart, and lean not on your own understanding; in all your ways acknowledge Him, and He shall direct your paths."

Don't lean on your own limited understanding; instead, in everything you do, trust Him, and He will direct you and greatly expand your ways. The ways may not be exactly as you envision them though … mostly because our timetable is shorter than God's, and we have a hard time waiting on God. However, His ways are always best.

Sometimes it seems like we are waiting and waiting. God seems distant, or maybe we think He set us aside as He deals with someone else. That, however, is simply *not* true. God is at work while we seem to be waiting. He teaches us things then, things such as patience, steadfastness, endurance and, of course, trust. Maybe He is allowing you (or others) to mature. Abraham never saw many of God's promises, yet he still maintained faith, as evidenced by his unwavering trust in God.

Are you willing to wait? If not, your faith will be inconsistent, and it may decrease by your own impatience. There are no shortcuts on God's path for you, yet it is the best possible path. Remember, God is awesome, powerful, smarter than you, knows what is ahead of you in life, and is compassionate and merciful!

That should give you peace. Trust is how we demonstrate our faith and proper hope, and I think it is also a prerequisite of peace.

FAITH PRODUCES PEACE

Faith involves hope and trust and then gives us peace. Those pinnacles of life are so closely related, but explicitly different. Even so, they are covered under faith as a way to glorify God. Faith starts the process toward the other three. Did you catch that progression?

True hope comes from faith, is demonstrated by trust, then brings us peace.

"God will keep you in perfect peace when your mind is stayed on Him," as Isaiah 26:3 says. I think the Holy Spirit helps us to have hope and peace, but it starts with us having faith. An old prophet of God said in Habakkuk 2:4, "the just shall live by his faith," which stuck in the mind of Martin Luther, who realized we don't have to do a bunch of works or pay money to be saved. We are saved when we have faith in the works of Jesus, not ours.

Paul probably was also thinking of Habakkuk 2:4 when he wrote

Therefore, having been justified by faith, we have peace with God through our Lord Jesus Christ, through whom also we have access by faith into this grace in which we stand, and rejoice in hope of the glory of God. And not only that, but we also glory in tribulations, knowing that tribulation produces perseverance; and perseverance, character; and character, hope. Now hope does not disappoint, because the love of God has been poured out in our hearts by the Holy Spirit who was given to us. (Rom. 5:1–5 NKJV)

Peace is that sense we get when through faith, hope, and trust, we have done all we can do *with* Him. Peace comes throughout. It guards our minds and hearts because of faith, hope, and trust in Him. Whatever happens to you, including the process, has been passed through the approving hands of God:

"[A]nd the peace of God, which surpasses all understanding, will guard your hearts and minds through Christ Jesus" (Phil. 4:7).

I love the use of the word "guard" in that verse. It is saying God's peace is like having a personal armed bodyguard who protects your mind and heart. That is a concept I really need to remind myself often … and I assume you do too.

What you have just read is a sequence, a thought pattern with practical applications to your daily life and well-being. So work on the sequence. Write it on a sticky note at your desk or on your bathroom mirror at home: Faith → Hope → Trust → Peace.

When we do those in that sequence, as Paul said in Romans 5:1–5, we *rejoice*; indeed, we even *glory* in tribulations. Wow! Faith is super important then, isn't it?! That's why having faith glorifies God!!

FAITH PRODUCES LOVE.

Genuine love is what Jesus was talking about when He was asked what the greatest commandment was: to love God, and then love others. It's actually is a product of proper and sincere faith.

The command to love God and others must include the truth or good news of the gospel; "gospel truth" is what some say. Faith in God embraces His love for others, which becomes our willing choice where others are more important than ourselves … that's how Jesus was. (And we will delve into that topic of love in the next chapter.)

First Timothy 1:5 says that love comes from a pure heart, from a good conscience, and from sincere faith. That's a faith in the Word of God. Faith must be sincere, which goes hand in hand with, and may be a prerequisite of, sincere love.

HELP FROM JAMES AND PETER

The book of James in the Bible is written by a half-brother of Jesus who didn't even pay much attention to Jesus until after He rose from the grave. James was a mega-church pastor in the church in Jerusalem.

James wrote his book before any others in the New Testament, probably because he had a target audience who needed immediate help. He had compassion for them because they were worn out, tired, suffering, and harassed by trials and mean-spirited people. Sound like you, sometimes?

James starts out right away penning this about faith in verse 2: "My brethren, count it all joy when you fall into various trials knowing the testing of your faith produces patience." He says trials come so you can find out how deep of a root your faith has, and when you do, and your faith remains intact, it is a joy to know that. That first chapter of James is a must read for helping you have more faith, and he tells you exactly how to have it and gain more: Endure through the temptations and don't waiver in your Christian beliefs.

James gives proof of the faith you do have in 2:14–26. Basically, doing good works, bearing fruit, and glorifying God in the sixteen ways in this book are proof of your faith. You have to be intentional, but proof will help you be confident and increase your faith.

James and Peter got to know each other a lot better after Jesus came back to life and went on to heaven. I am fairly sure they hung out together several times and talked about faith and how to gain more. Peter, a hard-working, practical kind of guy, someone we can relate to, carefully wrote down a to-do list of Christian living, which starts with faith. You can read it in 2 Peter 1:5–10.

He said to diligently add to your faith these things (in other words, give maximum effort), because when you do, you won't doubt your salvation, you make sure you won't fall away from Jesus, and you'll continue to have confidence you will get to heaven.

- *Virtue*: Deeds of moral excellence, gaining energy and purpose from Jesus.
- *Knowledge:* Diligent study of the Word of God. Because it's truth, you know how to respond to situations and news reports each day.
- *Self-control:* Holding yourself to God's moral standard and obeying Him, living in the Spirit instead of the flesh. Controlling your emotions. Remaining even-keeled and anchored to God's truth.
- *Perseverance:* Patience and endurance during trials and temptations. Always do what is right, never give in, and maintain your hope.
- *Godliness:* Being the image of Jesus, loyal to Him, holy (separate from the world's system), and obedient.
- *Brotherly kindness:* Brotherly love for others, even sacrificing for them like brothers should. Do kind things for others expecting nothing in return.
- *Love:* The greatest command of Jesus is to love God, and the second is to love others like you love yourself, both in terms of the feeling and your actions.

Peter didn't pull any punches when he said if you don't do these diligently, you are useless, fruitless, forgetful, unfaithful, and short-sighted ... some are even blind.

"SO IS BEING FAITHFUL THE RESULT OF HAVING FAITH?"

Being faithful is undoubtedly the goal if every Christian. The word "faithful" is mentioned well over 50 times in the New Testament alone, and the reason being faithful should be a Christian's goal is because God requires us to be faithful, and we are working to hear this phrase when we get to heaven: "Well done, good and *faithful* servant!"

How awesome will it be when we are faithful to God and are rewarded with that statement along with a hug from Jesus?! That is a wonderful goal to work for.

Being faithful sounds like being full of faith. It's more than that, however, and much more down to earth. It's being loyal, adhering firmly to Jesus and His Word. Being faithful is trusting what God says is true; in fact, you *rely* on that. Here is a good description of being faithful: being faithful is when your faith dictates your reality.

When your life is consistent with what you read in Scripture and what you know about God, you are faithful. Being faithful demonstrates your faith, and it actually grows your faith, just as exercising grows your endurance and strengthens your muscles. When you do something athletic or physical, you rely on your muscles, and they are faithful to you. Likewise, when we are faithful, God can rely on us to accomplish His will.

When you finally see Jesus, and He shakes your right hand firmly and clasps it with His other hand, looking right into your eyes and saying: "Well done, good and faithful servant," it is because you were useful and profitable to Him, spreading the good news of the gospel and accomplishing His will for you. Notice at the center of that usefulness is your being faithful. Hebrews 4:2 says the gospel did not profit a certain group of people because it was not mixed with faith.

We learn of Jesus' statement in His parable of the talents in Matthew 25. Those who were faithful in doing what their boss asked of them were rewarded with "Well done, good and faithful servant; you were faithful over a few things, I will make you ruler over many things. Enter into the joy of your lord." There are rewards for being faithful.

Faithfulness is a *requirement* for any meaningful and long-term relationship. You require your spouse to be faithful to you, not just in sexual faithfulness, but in all areas of the relationship.

When your spouse is faithful to you, it's because they are obedient to God, devoted to you, and because they love you. Very similarly, you should be devoted to God for basically the same three reasons. What did Jesus say were the greatest commandments in Matthew 22:36–40? To love God and to love others. That implies being faithful.

As an employer for many years, I found that the best employees, the ones who were most successful in their careers, were the ones that could be described as *faithful.* You should be faithful to your boss/employer in all ways and always. And being faithful and useful to Jesus translates to being successful as a Christian.

According to the Merriam-Webster Online Dictionary, "faithful" means steadfast in affection or allegiance, honest, loyal, adhering to promises or duty, true to facts, true to one's word, or true to a standard.[4]

- Are you loyal to your boss? How about to Jesus?
- Do you adhere to the standards your boss has set or to the company's employee handbook? To the Bible?
- Does your boss have confidence in you? Does Jesus?
- If your boss was asked about you, would he or she say you were faithful? Will Jesus say you were faithful when you get to heaven?

Your faithfulness to God means being filled with faith. It's how God measures our significance to Him. It does not matter how significant the thing is to God we are faithful doing. Hudson Taylor said, "A little thing is a little thing, but being faithful in a little thing, is a big thing!" Also, God knows we are not perfect, and our faith may stagger a bit at times, but it does not fall down. God is interested in our direction, not our perfection. Being faithful means your faith is steadfast, does not waiver, and *continually* glorifies God.

A little faith will bring your soul to heaven; a great faith will bring heaven to your soul.
—Charles Spurgeon

THE FAITH MUSEUM

Hebrews chapter 11 is known as the "Hall of Faith" in the Bible, and reading it is like going to a museum to learn about faith. Let me take you on an afternoon visit to the "Faith Museum":

You drive your car into a pothole-filled gravel parking lot and park it next to another car in a row. Your pastor suggested you visit the Faith Museum when you questioned your faith in his office just the day before. "I guess I don't even know what faith is, so I probably don't even have any," you said as he smiled and scribbled down an address on a piece of paper for you then added, "It'll be the best twenty dollars you will ever spend."

You get out of your car and notice a couple others pull into the lot, drive around aimlessly, and leave. As you stand there wondering caringly about those people, trying to wave them in to park next to you, a man with a "Faith Museum" badge pinned to his safety-yellow vest says to you, "The museum fee is twenty dollars; we take all forms ..." You had a twenty-dollar bill in your pocket and hand it to the man before he can finish his sentence.

Curiously, you notice a red bottle in his hand, then he uses it to mark your car windshield with a large, fat letter "C," which interestingly turns out white. You wonder if that's permanent, then remember your high school homecoming when you would write "Go Panthers!" on car windows with a similar bottle of white shoe polish. You are about to ask the parking attendant about that letter "C" when he blurts out, "The way to the museum is down a narrow path," nodding his head toward one edge of the parking lot as he moves on to the next newly parked car.

It takes some people a while to find the path, but you find it right away. The path twists and turns, but it is relatively smooth if you pay attention to just the lit path in front of you and avoid the weeds along the edges and potholes filled with stagnant rainwater. Just as you begin to wonder if there's really a museum at all, it appears, almost out of nowhere. You notice, draped across the top of a door, a makeshift large white banner with handwritten red letters, as if painted by a tired old man: "Now faith is the substance of things hoped for, the evidence of things not seen."

You assume this is the entrance and go through the door. Once inside the Faith Museum, you are greeted warmly by a joyful, elderly woman

with a name badge that brings a smile to your face. "Grandma" hands you
a booklet and mentions it has some helpful information and a place to write
notes, and she smiles as she points out it's printed to look like a Bible. When
you open it, right in the middle is a map of the museum on the right side
of the fold. You realize the building is the shape of a cross, and there are
several rooms to go through along the way. You notice each room is in an
"arm" of the cross. "Oh, how cool!" you say out loud.

It seems to be a self-guided tour, but you can always look at that booklet
in your hand which will help you along if you take a few minutes to study
it. "Grandma" said it's best to read it on a regular basis, to help maximize
your tour through the museum.

- The first room is in the "left arm" of the cross and is called "Faith
  in History." You notice there are several displays, and the first is an
  illuminated video screen.
  - Atop the screen is the statement "By faith, we understand the
    world was created by the Word of God and what you see in the
    world was made from things you can't see." The video shows a
    model of an atom, and you recall from high school we cannot
    see atoms because they are mostly empty space with a little tiny
    nucleus and an electron a long way from it. The video continues
    with a description of subatomic light particles and a description
    of energy, all with the stunning CGI graphics of a Hollywood
    blockbuster movie. There's a segment about quantum mechanics
    and even dark matter for those who are interested in that, but
    you aren't, so you move on.
  - Your eyes catch sight of a simple wooden chair. It looks as if
    a million people have sat on it, but it seems to remain sturdy.
    Next to the chair is a sign inviting you to "experience faith" by
    turning around and sitting down on the solid old chair. When
    you do and face the other way, you notice a sign you can only
    see when sitting in the chair. "The solid chair you're faithfully
    sitting on is made of 99.994 percent thin air. Those educated
    in atomic science would observe that data and never sit on the
    chair for fear of falling to the ground unsupported. Welcome

to faith, which solidly defies science! Please continue to the
next room."

- The next room has a sand-covered uneven floor and is called the
Hall of Ancient Men.
  - Abel is depicted in the first reader board you come to. It tells
  how he believed by faith what God required for an acceptable
  sacrifice and how his brother Cain didn't. Cain got so mad when
  he found out God didn't accept his faithless sacrifice, he killed
  his brother Abel. You remember the story as you move to the
  next reader board.
  - This one is about Enoch, who walked and talked with God, even
  though he couldn't see Him. God was so pleased with that kind
  of faith, He just brought him up to heaven. As your head tilts
  back to ponder the fact Enoch didn't die, you notice an illuminated revolving string of words above that leaves a memorable
  impression on you and other visitors: "But without faith, it is
  impossible to please God, for he who comes to God must believe
  that He is, and that He is a rewarder of those who diligently seek
  Him." It seemed like a silly advertisement at first, but just then
  someone hands each visitor what looks like a business card, but
  it just has white words on a black background: "Got Faith?"
  - As you look at the card and put it in your pocket, that person
  then motions for you to move along to the next reader board.
  It has a picture of the ark and the story about Noah and how
  even though it had never rained, he obeyed God with faith and
  built a huge boat over the course of about seventy-five years.[5]
  It describes faith as believing what God says. Noah believed
  what God said would happen way off in the future and that
  God would save Noah and his family, and Noah maintained
  his faith even though he was constantly ridiculed by people the
  whole time he was building a boat with no water anywhere near.
  You comment to the visitor next to you how you can relate to
  that kind of ridicule, and they nod back in agreement.

- You find yourself continuing clockwise around the museum following the flow of other visitors and come to the next room called the Hall of Abraham.
  - The first reader board here tells about how in faith, Abraham trusted God when he was told to leave where he was living and start walking to some foreign country, and God would tell him why and where to go later. So Abraham packed up all of his household stuff—and he had a lot of stuff—and just headed out even though God didn't tell him whay and where for a long time. The sketch on the reader board looks like quite a caravan of people, animals, and carts moving across a hot desert. In the sketch, there's a man (probably depicting Abraham) holding a compass with no needle. As you think to yourself, *There have been times in my life I had no direction or purpose,* you see the next reader board.
  - This one is actually attached to the first one and is smaller. It's about the faith Abraham had when God told him that where he was going, there would be a huge city on a hill, but that city hadn't been built yet.
  - As you follow the other visitors shuffling along the sandy floor, you come to a huge painting of Sarah. She was Abraham's elderly wife, who was stunningly beautiful, even for her age. Above her is an enlarged photograph of the stars in the night sky and another showing a vast sandy seashore. Confused and curious why these two photographs are there, you notice the reader board beneath them saying both she and Abraham had faith when God told them their descendants would be as numerous as the stars in the sky and as the grains of sand on a seashore … but Sarah couldn't have kids. She still had faith it would happen. "Oh yeah! She was barren!" you blurt out loud, quickly covering your mouth with embarrassment as you look to make a quick exit from the room.
  - You *do* find the exit, which is also the entrance to another room. But as you head through, you see it's a set of very narrow gates and a screen just above them saying Sarah and Abraham never saw the big city they were told was going to be their home, and

they never saw the multitude of their descendants, but they still had faith in "what was to come." As you squeeze through those gates, offering barely enough room for one person to fit through, you notice they are "pearly gates" and smile at the implication.

- Just through those gates, you take a quick look at your map of the museum and see the next room is called the Hall of the Patriarchs. You confirm your bearings when you see from the map this is in the "right horizontal arm" of the cross.

  - As you enter this Hall of the Patriarchs, you first see a statue of Abraham with a knife in his hand, ready to plunge it into the heart of his only son, Isaac, and there is even a male sheep standing behind Abraham in some sticks and bushes. "Oh yeah, I remember that story!" you say out loud ... and are hushed by the visitor next to you. The writing below the statue tells how Abraham knew God promised him a multitude of descendants, and when his old and barren wife Sarah actually did have a son, Abraham had faith God would still fulfill His promise even though God had told him to kill Isaac. A very impactful story of faith, but what you saw next sent a shiver up your spine. As you walked away from that awesome display of faith, you saw an eerie shadow on the wall behind, coming from the statue of Abraham and Isaac. It seemed to also integrate the lamb in the back of the statue, but the shadow on the wall is of another Son being killed on a wooden cross.

  - When you turn away from that shadow, stunned with the reality of the typology depicted, you notice a series of plaques on the wall, one right after another. The first is about Isaac, then Jacob, then Rahab, Sampson, and a few others, including Joseph. Each tells about the faith they had. Joseph's plaque had a small crowd of visitors paused around it, commenting on how he maintained faith even when a lot of bad things happened to him. "People sure relate to Joseph," you whisper to the visitor next to you.

  - At the end of the row of plaques is a tabletop display of Jericho, the huge stone-walled city that crumbled to the ground at the sound of trumpets. You walk all the way around the display considering how painstaking this complex display must have been to put together. You notice it even has little toy soldiers circling the city with their horns instead of weapons. You can push a little red button next to several of the soldiers and hear them describe what they saw and did. Each story ends with enlightening statements about their newfound faith in the power of God and how they will never again doubt God and always believe and obey Him from then on!

◦ After circling the Jericho display several times, maybe even seven, making sure you pushed every button, you move on to the end of this Hall of Patriarchs, but what first catches your eye are padded chairs in front of a small theater screen. You welcome the chance to sit down and rest a bit. You sit back and exhale with relief as you stretch out your legs under the chair in front of you. The lights dim, and a video presentation starts showing on the screen. It's about Moses and starts out like the movie *The Ten Commandments*. As you crave popcorn and a soft drink, you realize it's not that movie, however, but it does show some events and actual discoveries proving the exodus out of Egypt and the Israelites' time in the wilderness did take place.

The actual videos of chariot wheels at the bottom of the Red Sea were astonishing to see! The film centers on the faith of Moses, giving example after example. It's fascinating, and you whisper to yourself, *I hope this doesn't end soon; I sure like this chair.* The movie does end, the lights rise, and you have to get up and move along with the other visitors toward the next room in the museum. Your legs stiffened up a little while sitting, but it does feel good to get moving again.

• As you exit the video room, you see a large clay pot with the words "For God" written on it. Some visitors go right on by, pretending they didn't see the pot, probably assuming it's a donation jar, but something tells you to slow down and pause there. Next to the pot is a notepad and pen. You are encouraged to write down things you worry about or wish for on the notepad, tear that sheet off, and "give them to God." When you place your notes in the pot, you hear a deep voice say,

"I will take care of that for you. Commit, believe, and live abundantly!" Your eyes widen, and your jaw drops as you look up, wondering if you would see a speaker, maybe even God, but just as you do, a museum attendant lightly grabs your elbow and ushers you along to the next room, leaning in close to your left ear and softly asking: "After doing that, do you feel the peace that surpasses understanding?" Tears well up in your eyes as you smile and nod in agreement.

- Then you come to a circular room and think, *This must be the center of the cross-shaped museum.* A quick look at your map of the museum confirms you're correct. As you enter the room, there's a statue of Moses with Jesus standing right next to him. This statue is in the middle of the room, and carved into the foundation around Moses' worn sandals are these words: "For he endured as seeing Him who is invisible." As you marvel at seeing Jesus in the statue, you overhear comments from other visitors that this is central to having a strong faith. Sadly, others mumble they don't see Jesus there, only Moses, and head out of the room.

- You follow after them, wanting to help them see Jesus, but there's suddenly a lot of excitement. Visitors are handed a free backpack! It's a beautiful looking backpack and fits each visitor comfortably. Inside are a lot of things, heavy things, so the excitement only increases as to what wonderful things may be inside! Everyone heads down a very long hallway, and a museum attendant says, "It leads to the last room of the museum—no running allowed." You don't need to look at your map to know this long hallway is the "lower part of the cross."

Your backpack becomes very heavy, and you realize it's making you tired and weary. You decide to see what's in it, contemplating throwing off some of whatever is in there to lighten the load. To your surprise, it's full of heavy rocks with a word written on each one. "Bitterness," "Wrath," "Anger," "Clamor," "Evil Words," "Lying," "Coveting," "Worry," "Hate," "Sexual Immorality," "Remorse," "Unforgiveness," and some others. You notice these rocks are exactly the same size each. As you stop and fall to your knees, you are overcome with the weight of each and the need to put each one far away from you. You look around at the other visitors and see many of them are also getting weary, but some continue on ahead getting angry, even cussing out loud as they plod along. You notice the familiar famous sepia-colored painting of Jesus and then, with blurring eyes, see a "Roman Road" up to the painting with words written on each paver in the road. The words are becoming unclear as you make out just a few, maybe even incorrectly, but they give you some hope as you try to understand them. You soon realize these words convey that we all have these sins, and with them you will fall short of the best exit out of the museum unless you repent of these sins and lay them under that painting of Jesus. You blurt out, "I'm sorry for lying to my brother when we were kids," as you lay down the rock called "Lying"; "I'm sorry I hated my neighbor when they got their new car," as you lay down the rock "Coveting"; and you continue until all the rocks are gone. You notice a sign on the floor right there at your knees saying "Your *faith* in Jesus saved you from the burden and penalty of those sins."

You stand up, looking at that painting of Jesus, which seems to give you rest, then a feeling of total rejuvenation fills you! You didn't see it before, but now you notice clouds along the walls of this long hallway with faces in the clouds whose eyes seem to follow you as you start to walk along. They're not creepy or overpowering, but somehow uplifting and encouraging. The faces have some sort of name badges under them, names such as Gideon, Samson, David, Samuel, Elijah, Jeremiah, and Daniel. With newfound energy, you continue down this hallway and are excited to see a series of small free-standing signs. They are arranged so you have to weave around each one like slalom gates in an Olympic skiing event. That makes it fun to read each one quickly as you zoom by to the next one timed with your quickly paced steps:

- "Your faith has saved you."
- "Faith is accepting what God gives, whether you agree with Him or not."
- "Faith is your response to what God has said."

- "Faith leads to life!"
- "Faith connects God's Word with reality."
- "Faith doesn't create an obstacle out of what you don't know, but is accepting what you do know."
- "Faith doesn't always change your circumstances, but faith is still faith in God's eyes."
- "Faith is when you choose to suffer affliction with God's people rather than to enjoy the passing pleasures of sin."

You are having fun and hope you can remember them, but you keep going …
- "Don't get your theology from your circumstances."
- "Don't judge God by your circumstances."
- "Don't let your circumstances change the joy you have in Jesus."
- "Faith realizes the trials God allows are proof of His love."
- "Faith realizes Jesus is with you always. You and Jesus are a perfect team."
- "Faith is not giving up. Even when it's dark, He's teaching you patience and trust."

You pause for a moment after that one. You then take a few deep breaths and continue on as you see the next one:

- "Keep going; you're almost there!"
- "Faith sees His grace is sufficient."
- "Faith is realizing God's ways are better than your ways."
- "Faith is not being ashamed to say 'I follow Jesus.'"
- "You cannot please God without faith."
- "You will attain a good testimony through faith."
- "Faith is believing God will keep His promises."
- "Faith always, *always* leads to ultimate victory!"

A little tired, but excited about all you just read, you remember the card you were handed earlier and pull it out of your pocket to read again: "Got faith?" Tears well up in your eyes as you clench that card to your chest as a prized possession, then put it back in your pocket for safekeeping.

Continuing to think about all of those signs, wishing you had a book with them all written down, you walk along this long hallway and notice the lights in the museum are behind you. It's very dark ahead of you, and there are no direction arrows, not even a red "EXIT" sign. There's no one else around, so you walk faster; you think that maybe you just need to catch up, as your breathing increases.

The faster pace is making you exhausted, and it doesn't seem to be doing any good. The next exhibit should be ahead, but you suddenly feel alone, and it's dark. Your mind drifts to the tasks you have to do at home … mow the lawn, put the dishes away, and watch the next season of your favorite show on DVR. You become impatient and frustrated. This long dark hallway is much longer than you thought. Maybe you made a wrong turn; maybe you shouldn't have even come to this museum. "Hello? Is anyone there?" you blurt out loud. No response. Not even an echo.

Abandoned and tired, you pause. In fact, you slump to your knees, and tears well up in your eyes as you mutter softly, "Where is everyone? This sucks. Where … is … God?!" You just stay there, down on the floor, and your teeth begin to clench together angrily. "I want my twenty bucks back," you mutter out loud with teeth still clenched. "I trust there's a return policy."

One of those words you just muttered in frustration sticks in your mind … trust. *Trust!*

You cannot see the museum map shaped like a Bible because it's too dark, but you remember it enough to recall this hallway is very long, the lower part of the "cross." And, one of those little signs way back behind you said something about learning patience and *trust* when life sends you trials or seems dark. Is this all part of the Faith Museum?

You get up, holding your map in front of you as if you can sense which way to go through the unseen paper. Your other hand grasps that little "Got Faith?" card still in your pocket. And you start walking. You say to yourself, *I'm sorry Father; I trust you, even if I have to walk for a long, long time.*

Just then, for some strange reason, the thought of a battered and injured Jesus carrying the heavy cross up the hill on Good Friday all those years ago came to your mind, and you keep walking, thinking about Him … thanking Him.

- The lights seem to get brighter, and you finally come near the end of that long hallway and enter what must be the last room of the Museum of Faith. You think this must be the foot of the cross as you look at the map in the new light, is the map a bit crumpled due to your tight grip on it in the dark time. It *is* the foot of the cross, and it's a simple room, and you even notice some people just go through it quickly and noisily. You are excited and even giddy to be there, but you hear a museum attendant off to one side whisper, "Be still," so you obey. Then you also hear a voice whispering, "If you do, you'll be overwhelmed with a sense of God multiplying your faith."

  ◦ Only when you are still and quiet do you hear the unmistakable song of a meadowlark, smell pine in the air as from a fresh Christmas tree, and see the pinkish-orange pastel alpenglow of a new morning sunrise. Looking for the source of that sunrise with a growing smile, your eyes are drawn to an amazingly realistic 3D hologram of a vivid colorful rainbow over the most beautiful scenery on earth.

    The same soft-spoken museum attendant asks each person who did pause, "Come closer; what does this mean to you?" As you and the others gather in around the hologram on some sort of round table, someone says the rainbow gives them a reminder of God's promises. Another person says the evidence of God can be clearly seen in the majesty of the mountains, trees, waterfalls, animals, and colorful clouds of the sunrise. Several others look a little more intently into the hologram and, moving in closer, they say they can see far off in the distance a city on a hill. It seems to be a mixture of glass and colorful gemstones, with golden streets.

    You also move a little closer with squinting eyes to make the scene clearer. Collectively, as if all just hit a casino jackpot at the same time, everyone, including you, shouts with elation, "Look!" and several point to a man who can be seen through the glass walls sitting on a throne in the glimmering city. The man has a crown, is wearing a blood-stained white robe, and there's something else … something very unmistakable: scars on His hands. Several people in unison seem to melt to their knees as if overcome with emotion … and so do you.

○ As everyone keeps looking, unable to quit staring at the King on the throne, someone says, "I sure wish I could talk to Him." Just then, a large dark purple curtain at the end of the room seems to tear open from top to bottom. Through the curtain shines a bright light. To some, it was just the very bright sunlight of the outdoors, because their eyes had adjusted to the darker light of the museum.

However, many visitors, yourself included have a different idea about the light, as all eyes fill with tears of joy. You all congregate with an unmentioned commonality as you all slowly make your way through the curtain–sided exit toward the light. The group of people now around you are saying out loud what's on each of their minds: "I *can* talk to Him," "Yahweh is real," "My King!" "It's joyous," "What we read in Revelation is real!" Some say just one thoughtful word such as "Truth," "Love," and "Hope." You realize where you are and notice your parked car just as you gently slap your chest pocket and thoughtfully choose your own words to likewise blurt out: "Got faith."

Returning to your car, you open the driver's door, and sit down partly in, with one leg still out of the car. You cannot bring yourself to start it and drive away because your mind is swirling with thoughts as you want to keep the experience going.

You notice the "C" on the windshield from your seat inside the car, and with the door still open, stand up and reach around with your left hand to wipe it away. But after just a couple wipes at it, you realize you cannot reach it all, so you just sit back down and exhale loudly, as if exhausted from the effort. In fact, you just sit there for quite some time, staring through the windshield, through the backward "C," lost in thought.

You learned about faith while at the museum, but that's not what you are thinking about. The last word you heard someone say, "Hope," is as fresh on your mind as the image of King Jesus on His throne (which was as real to you as the steering wheel now in your hands). Oh, how you long to see Him there for real.

The phrase "gather your thoughts" doesn't occur to you, but the word "hope" and the image of the live presence of Jesus in His Glory, are indelibly there. Oh, and that backward "C"? With all your earlier attempts to wipe it off, it now looks more like an arrow pointing to the right from your perspective inside of the car. Just then, the gathering of your thoughts happens: Hope → Jesus.

Suddenly, hope pointing to Jesus is vivid to you. Your hope of seeing Jesus on His throne and the reality of 100 percent certainty He will be there soon come together in one word … and you blurt that word out loud resoundingly from inside your car as you close the door with a smile, nod your head, and start the engine: "*Faith!!!*"

PRACTICAL APPLICATIONS

1. Increase your faith by keeping a thanks diary, so you can keep and recall the many times God has answered your prayers and proven Himself trustworthy and faithful so you can trust Him on current and future issues.

2. _____

_____

3. _____

_____

3 LOVE

Love is what it's all about. Seriously, love of God and love of others should be the obvious defining attribute of every true Christian. It's the defining attribute of God ... and it brings glory to Him when we love.

LOVE IS A COMMAND ... AND FOR GOOD REASON!

One of the best teaching sessions for Christians is John chapters 14 and 15. In John 15 verse 12, Jesus said, "This is My commandment, that you love one another as I have loved you." To make sure we got it, He repeated it again in verse 17. In fact, the central theme of this whole passage is to love God and love others. With John 14:15, Jesus tells us if we love Him, we will keep His commandments, further solidifying love is our central life theme. It's hard to do in our world today, I know, but maybe that's why Jesus wanted us to be lights in a dark world ... maybe love is the light?

While studying this way to glorify God, I found the word "love" occurs 365 times in the Bible. Isn't that interesting! 365 days in a year... 365 times of love in the Bible. Light of the sun shines on the earth 365 times in one year, and so should love from you toward others.

When I read the Gospel of John, and also his small book 1 John, the word "love" jumps out at me, because he uses it often. I think the impact

Jesus made on John can be summed up in one word … love. John was very intelligent and realized love is what it's all about. We should too. The most quoted passage in all the Bible is John 3:16, and what is its theme? "For God so loved the world …" By the way, those aren't John's words—it's a quote from Jesus.

Paul echoes John, who learned from Jesus, in 1 Corinthians 13:13. In fact, right after telling us what love is, what love is not, and how to love, he delivered his famous top-three traits of a true Christian: "And now abide faith, hope, love, these three; but the greatest of these is love."

In Matthew 22:33–39, Jesus had just astonished people with His incredible teaching, so one of the most intelligent guys, a lawyer, who had determined there were 613 commandments of God from the Pentateuch, hoped to stump or possibly trap Jesus. He asked Him what the greatest command was. Jesus answered, "To love God with all your heart, soul, and mind." He quickly added, "[T]he second is like it, to love your neighbor as yourself." That close-second command that places the best interest of others equal to your own is a great character trait to have, because it shows love for others.

The passage above was documented by Matthew, who previously was a tax collector and hated by almost everyone. You can picture this sort of guy, a crooked, arrogant, haughty IRS agent who audits you and charges you more taxes than what you know you are supposed to owe, plus double interest, and threatens to take your house, your car, and garnish your wages, just because he can. He knows everyone hates him, and he lives for it … he takes pleasure in ruining people.

That was Matthew. Then Jesus came along and showed him love … and Matthew quit his job immediately and followed Jesus. He was so impressed by the fact that Jesus would love him that he invited him over to his house for dinner (along with some other crooked IRS guys) … and Jesus *went*! Jesus loved them too … something most of us would have a hard time doing.

Just in case you are thinking, "Yeah, but there are some people I cannot love," remember God loves the world (and everyone in it), so much so that He sent His own Son (John 3:16) to pay the penalty of sins out of love for them … even for those guys who beat and whipped Him (1

John 1:9). Loving one another is a command from Jesus, pointed directly at us Christians: "A new commandment I give to you, that you love one another; as I have loved you, that you also love one another. By this all will know that you are My disciples, if you have love for one another" (John 13:34–35).

So, since love is so important, what does love actually mean? We really need to understand this!

"WHAT IS LOVE, ANYWAY?"

The New Testament was written in Greek. I know just enough of the Greek language to wish I knew more. It does a better job of explaining things through unique words that our English language does not have. The Greeks were not lazy when it came to words. We English-speaking types can be lazy with words and too often hope the context conveys the meaning. One example is the word "love." Consider these uses of the word love: "I love my truck," "I love my mom," "I want to make love," "I love hunting," "I love the people in our church," "I love you, man!" and, "I love my wife." All use the same English word "love," but if you don't know the context or the person speaking, you could greatly misinterpret the statement. However, in Greek, there are six specific words for love:

- *Ludus*, a playful love of things or persons, less serious than other words for love
- *Philautia*, the love of the self
- *Philia*, a deep friendship, or brotherly love
- *Pragma*, a longstanding love
- *Eros*, a sexual or passionate love
- *Agape*, a love for people as God does

All of these bring glory to God in their rightful setting, but one in particular, I think, does more than the others: Agape. This word "agape" rarely appears in any Greek literature; however, it is written over two hundred times in the New Testament. That tells me it's a concept that may be uniquely Christian. Therefore, we should pay very close attention to it and learn to express that kind of love. Doing so more expressively brings glory to God.

I think the apostle John grasped the meaning of the agape type of love more than any of the forty biblical writers, and through the writing of his books, the Holy Spirit taught us how to love each other. First John 3:14 tells us that life is centered in love: "We know that we have passed from death to life, because we love the brethren. He who does not love his brother abides in death."

John got this, and tied together the words "love" and "life" from Jesus when He was talking about us being like sheep in John 10:1–18 and Jesus as a good shepherd. In verse 10, Jesus said, "I have come that they [us sheep who call Jesus our shepherd] may have life, and that they may have it to the full." A life that is full and abundant is a life that loves others and that glorifies God.

Notice in the 1 John 3:14 passage the words "brethren" and "brother." Those mean fellow people, not just your familial brother. Life is lived more fully and is more glorifying to God when we love others with a love that *does*, not just a love that is. Love wants the best for others, does what is best for others, seeks justice for those who are oppressed, and brings the light and mission of Jesus to their lives.

Love wears shoes, and those shoes are called "grace."

"Then how do I love? Isn't it just a feeling?"

The books of 1 John; Ephesians 4, 5, and 6; and reading how Jesus interacted with others in Mark will help you put shoes and blue jeans on when it comes to loving others. Love is much more than a feeling, it's something you *do*. John says love is deeds in truth from the heart.

You glorify God by showing love toward others as Jesus did, and the way that jumps out at me when reading the gospels is Jesus' *compassion* and how He *served* others. Serving others brings out humility and puts away self-centeredness. It is "selfless." Be the first to volunteer to help others, organize events, and ask others about how they are doing—and really mean it by listening to their answer. Genuinely care about others, and show it by doing things for them. Serving others opens the door to other ways to show love as Jesus did, such as grieving with them when they are hurt and rejoicing with them when they experience joy. That also means celebrating their victories when good things happen.

In the gospel accounts of Jesus feeding the five thousand, they say He looked upon the multitudes and had *compassion* for them, for they were harassed and helpless. They were sick, hurting, and weary, like sheep without a shepherd. He then healed them, helped them, encouraged them, and fed them. What an awesome display of love to emulate! Love started inside of Him (compassion) and then became tangible (the deeds). We glorify Him when we do the same.

John chapter 15 is what I call the "Glorify God" chapter. Jesus teaches us how to glorify Him by being branches off of the vine (Jesus), through accepting His love and expressing love to others, by living joyfully, and through suffering for Him in a world He has overcome. Love is right in the middle of that. That's probably intentional, because love is central to being a Christian and to glorifying God.

We all know 1 Corinthians 13 is the love chapter, and just as there are sixteen ways to glorify God, there are sixteen ways to love others! I hope you know these are ways for Christians to love one another, not for just how to love our spouse. Let's review them, because loving one another is central to glorifying God. And remember, the key to love is being selfless. Selfless love is the priority for every Christian who glorifies God:

1. *Selfless love is patient.*
   We show others love by being patient with them, for a very long time. In fact, patience is listed first because it is the greatest way others can tell if we have love.
2. *Selfless love is kind.*
   Being kind means nice, caring, and compassionate. This includes empathy (bearing another's burden *with* them) and sympathy (relating a similar struggle in *unity*).
3. *Selfless love is not jealous.*
   Jealousy of what others have is the sin of coveting. Love is being happy for others when something good happens to them.
4. *Selfless love does not brag.*
   Don't make yourself look good at the expense of someone else.

5. *Nor is selfless love arrogant.*

   Arrogance is "I'm better than you," which is not love. Don't talk about what you have done ... love is other-centered, not self-centered. The silent treatment is not love.

6. *Selfless love does not act unbecomingly.*

   Being rude and selfish, yelling, and so on is not loving. Neither is talking negatively behind another's back.

7. *Selfless love does not seek its own.*

   Don't look out for yourself; look out for others first and treat them with honor and respect. You don't *always* have to win.

8. *Selfless love is not provoked.*

   Don't be easily angered. The situation does not dictate the whole. Love respects "no" and yields.

9. *Selfless love does not take into account a wrong suffered.*

   Don't keep track of past wrongs. Forgive and forget.

10. *Selfless love does not rejoice in unrighteousness.*

    Gloating when others stumble is not love; instead, love is compassionate and caring, helping others to get better. Love overlooks faults. Love never says "I told you so." But it does say "How can I help you through this?"

11. *Selfless love rejoices with the truth.*

    Truth rules, not hearsay. Rejoice when others stand for truth, even if it hurts them or you.

12. *Selfless love bears all things.*

    Selfless love puts up with a lot of stuff and overlooks annoyances. Love is lighthearted and answers softly. Love errs on the side of grace.

13. *Selfless love trusts.*

    The assured reliance on the character, ability, strength, and truthfulness of the other.

14. *Selfless love believes all things.*

    It actively looks for good things and dwells on the positive, not the negative, believing the best about others.

15. *Selfless love hopes all things.*

    Selfless love seeks and expects better things to come, including Christ's ability to change lives ... for the better. Love is about direction, not perfection.

16. *Selfless love endures all things.*

And that means *all* the hard things—sickness, lack of wealth, imperfections, getting walked on, passed over, unappreciated, and so on. Remember to put others first.

MONSTERS IN THE CLOSET NEED LOVE TOO.

Years ago, I didn't want to see the 2001 Pixar Animation Studios movie *Monsters, Inc.* However, I went anyway and was glad I did. The "monsters in the closet" were scary and real to little children; however, as the movie unfolds, you realize those monsters are not really fiends to be avoided; they're creatures with regular lives, families, and feelings. They're simply trying to make a living in their world. Get this: they thought people like you and me were monsters. In fact, as you get to know those characters, you become sympathetic to their struggles, maybe even share a little empathy with them, and possibly even learn to love them. As I walked to the car after seeing the movie, I wondered to myself, *Who are the monsters to me?*

When most of us were young, our parents taught us to beware of certain types of people, especially if our parents were Christians. Strangers, drinkers, tattooed bikers, politicians, tax collectors, those from a different culture or even a different orientation, those in the other political party … sound a bit familiar? These people—and others—might have been *your* monsters as a kid. Our parents' intention was protection. However, when we became adults, some of us retained that perception—that somewhat irrational fear of "others"—in our heads. We may have even escalated it to a graceless disdain for them, refusing to be sympathetic to their struggles or empathetic to their plight. As for love? That's out of the question! Conversely, "those other people's" view of Christians may come from that disdain that some even inflate to hate, and it's wrong for us to perpetuate that error. In other words, some people think *we* are a monster.

Jesus loves all people, even people kids were taught to avoid, and when He was on the earth, those people were drawn to Him. They could sense His love and more than a little understanding. They also could sense His willingness to forgive them, and they had hope in Him for a better life.

It's interesting the religious leaders of the day ridiculed Jesus for showing those people some grace (Matt. 9:11–12).

Everyone sins. Some are reactions to life's hardships and unfairness, or as Jesus said in John 16:33, "In this life, you will have tribulations." Some sins stem from bad choices or rebellion. But my point is all sins are equally horrible in the eyes of God, and we all have sinned, even you and me. We can all have our slate wiped clean freely by God's grace through the redemption that came by Christ Jesus (Rom. 3:23–24). And that includes those people your parents avoided.

We *all* need Jesus to take away the penalty of those sins. He is the only way, and He even called Himself a metaphorical "physician to the sick." To snobbishly single out others or their sins and think any of them are unworthy of what Jesus did for them on the cross is myopic, unloving, and very distasteful behavior. Grow up, and show a little of Jesus' grace and love to your "monsters" … you may just find they're not so different from you after all.

Jesus calls them "neighbors" and commands us to love our neighbors as ourselves, which is the second greatest commandment. When asked to define "neighbor," He described the good Samaritan in Luke 10:25–37. I'm sure you recall the story, which sets up a brilliant plot twist: A description of a "monster" … someone whom you were taught to avoid and wouldn't normally love … is your neighbor. Jesus knew that would be hard, so He told us very succinctly how to love your neighbor: Love them as you love yourself. Think about that.

Jesus so loves people—*all* people, including those who are "not normally loved"—so much, He died on the cross for them. The least you can do is let them feel welcome in your (Jesus') church, pray for them, or have coffee with them. They need compassion, forgiveness, and a better life from Jesus just like you did, and it's difficult for them to find Him without your showing them love.

You don't have to become one of them, and you don't have to change them … that's God's job! Just show them a little grace, a little compassion or empathy (love), and let them see the life-changing good news of Christ in you … they may want to experience it too. In *Monsters Inc.*, Sully (the monster) and Boo (the child) grew to care for each other and helped each other through life's struggles.

You can help someone in much the same way. And that will make Jesus smile … as you glorify Him.

LOVE HAS AN AROMA.

We have an "aroma" about us, something people sense when we are around. In fact, the aroma has a name. It's called love: "Therefore be imitators of God as dear children. And walk in love, as Christ also has loved us and given Himself for us, an offering and a sacrifice to God for a sweet-smelling aroma." (Eph. 5:1–2).

The Bible tells us in many passages that God is love, and we are to love others because Christ first loved us. So, there in Jesus is the *source* and *example* of love. Jesus was certainly a "know-it-all," but He didn't act like it. What drew people to Him was His love. He demonstrated it in ways such as concern, compassion, understanding, grace, help, and advice, none of which were judgmental or "lorded" over anyone. Oh, if we could be like Jesus … if we could love like Him, the world would be different. Even Facebook would be heartening, not disheartening.

We all know people who think they know everything … and we don't like to be around them. But we also know of people who are gracious toward others and love others … them, we like to hang around. And if they do have great knowledge, then we like them even more because we become better around them or because of them. Love trumps knowledge, and without love, knowledgeable people aren't as smart as they think they are. Paul knew this and told the people so in the church in Corinth: "Knowledge puffs up, but love builds up. The man who thinks he knows something does not yet know as he ought to know" (1 Cor. 8:1–2).

"They'll Know We Are Christians by Our Love." Remember that song from years ago? It was written by Peter Raymond Scholtes, probably as a response to 1 Peter 4:8: "And above all things have fervent love for one another, for love will cover a multitude of sins."

Popular author and speaker (and my cousin) Preston Sprinkle adds this, which is so relevant to showing the priority of love and grace of Jesus over "rules and religiousness": "The word 'Christian' is in the Bible three times; the word 'disciple' is there two hundred ninety-seven times. May we all repent from the creative ways we've pushed others away from Jesus by erecting man-made standards of righteousness."

LOVE LOOKS LIKE THIS.

Just as a grapevine has branches that shoot off it, there are several offshoots of love. They are recognizable things so you know what love looks like. Here are a few:

- *Patience.* Patience toward someone, or longsuffering (suffering for a long time), is an offshoot of love. It's simply love for God and love for others. Impatient people are lovers of themselves in a negative way. Patience is something we have to learn. It is a mark of a mature Christian that glorifies God. Unfortunately, patience is usually learned the hard way: "My brethren, count it all joy when you fall into various trials, knowing that the testing of your faith produces patience. But let patience have its perfect work, that you may be perfect and complete, lacking nothing" (James 1:2–4).

  I am so happy God is patient. A loving God and a loving person have a lot of patience … neither gives up soon or gets angry soon. So many times in my life, I knew my dad or my wife loved me because they were patient with me … allowing me to blow off steam or letting me have my own way to the point I knew I was wrong and was embarrassed about it. But their patience blew me away with the vision of their true love: *Love* → *Patience*

  Being patient while suffering through a rough period in my life has always resulted in good things. It has strengthened a relationship and my trust in God. "Be always humble, gentle, and patient. Show your love by being tolerant with one another" (Eph. 4:2 GNB).

- *Forgiveness.* It could be considered one of the root ways to glorify God, but it is actually an offshoot of love. Love for God and love for others is exemplified when we forgive those who have wronged us: "For God so loved the world that He gave His only begotten Son, that whoever believes in Him should not perish but have everlasting life" (John 3:16).

  See, because of God's love, He provided a sacrifice to facilitate forgiveness. Forgiveness starts with love: Love → Forgiveness

Forgiving others is a way to glorify God, but we do so out of love for Him and, by extension, our love for others. We are told—no, we are *commanded*—in Ephesians 4:32—5:2 to walk in love as a practical application in our daily life and to *forgive* others as God forgave us through Christ. This passage is in Paul's teaching on not only what to quit doing in our lives but also what to do a whole lot more of! Loving and forgiving others are the main ones: "And be kind to one another, tenderhearted, forgiving one another, even as God in Christ forgave you. Therefore be imitators of God as dear children. And walk in love, as Christ also has loved us and given Himself for us."

- *Meekness*—which is not *weakness*. Meekness is knowing your place before God and before others, and not stepping out of that place. The Greek word for meek means "tame." Picture a tame house cat versus an untamed lion. A synonym for meekness is *humble*. Humility before God and others takes great strength and maturity.

Jesus was meek but was one of the strongest men I can think of. He was a carpenter who slept in the wilderness, and how many guys did it take to tackle him when He overturned the money changers table? Zero. He was too strong, He had physical power. Yet He remained meek because He loved God and loved others. This is why God wants us to be meek or humble, and we do so because we love Him and love others: Love → Humility.

Humility is the opposite of pride. Pride is a sin that God hates, probably because it's the sin that got ahold of Lucifer when he fell (read about it in Isaiah 14:12–17 and Ezekiel 28:17–19). Love for God and love for people accurately manifests itself in our humility, and God will make sure humble people are exalted is His presence. "For the LORD takes delight in his people; he crowns the humble with victory" (Ps. 149:4).

"Blessed are the meek, for they will inherit the earth" (Matt. 5:5).

I am persuaded that love and humility are the highest attainments in the school of Christ and the brightest evidences that He is indeed our Master.
—John Newton

- *Others-centered.* Self-centeredness and selfishness are not glorifying to God, but being others-centered is: Love ➔ Others-centered.

  Others-centeredness is the opposite of self-centeredness. Love works best and is genuine when it comes from an other-centered heart with no personal motives. Doing so takes effort, even some faith, which is manifested in trusting God. Consider this verse, and notice the words "grace" and "faith": "For I say, through the grace given to me, to everyone who is among you, not to think of himself more highly than he ought to think, but to think soberly, as God has dealt to each one a measure of faith" (Rom. 12:3).

  Out of love for others, we can do this: "Let nothing be done through selfish ambition or conceit, but in lowliness of mind let each esteem others better than himself. Let each of you look out not only for his own interests, but also for the interests of others" (Phil. 2:3–4).

- *Care for others.* Out of love for God and others, we care for others, which is an action word. Empathy is another word to consider. We show our love for God when we do things or care for (pay attention to and meet the needs of) others: *Love ➔ Care for others*

  "Be kind to one another, tender-hearted, forgiving each other, just as God in Christ also has forgiven you" (Eph. 4:32).

  Care for others is showing them grace, which involves forgiving them. It is also being compassionate toward others, encouraging them, comforting them, going alongside and putting your arm around them, and sharing their burdens—or at least trying to go through the burden with them: "Bear one another's burdens, and thereby fulfill the law of Christ" (Gal. 6:2).

  In case we don't know whom to care for or how, James gives us some guidance:

  "Pure and undefiled religion before God and the Father is this: to visit orphans and widows in their trouble, and to keep oneself unspotted from the world" (James 1:27).

- *Encourage others.* Out of love for God and others, we encourage others. We show our love for God when we uplift the people God also loves. It is part of being in the family of God: Love ➔ Encourage others.

"And let us consider one another in order to stir up love and good works, not forsaking the assembling of ourselves together, as is the manner of some, but exhorting one another, and so much the more as you see the Day approaching" (Heb. 10:24–25).

Meeting together with other Christians is important, partly because you can be encouraged by others, but you can also encourage *others*. The times in life when you need encouragement the most are also the times you don't want to go to church or small group Bible study. It's interesting that happens isn't it?! But the best way, according to God's plan for His children whom He loves, is to gather with other believers and be encouraged.

Encouraging others should be a goal of every Christian who wants to glorify God because it does just that.

As Romans 12:9 tells us, love must be sincere. Others can quickly tell if your love is fake, and so can God, who is not glorified by false love. The world's love is self-centered and not sincere. God's love is other-centered. Love God's way. Love for others is not natural for us. In fact, we have to be intentional and put forth an effort to love others. And, as we all know, some people take a lot more effort than others, correct?

Our love to God is measured by our everyday fellowship with others and the love it displays.
—Andrew Murray

LOVE HAS GOODWILL.

We see the term *goodwill* several places in Scripture, and the more I looked into it, the more I realized it is an outpouring of our heart of love toward others, which brings glory to God.

I'm sure you recall the first place you saw this term in the Bible: You hear it each Christmas. It was spoken by the angel and repeated by a great multitude of the heavenly host in Luke 2:14: "Glory to God in the highest, And on earth peace, goodwill toward men!" They were announcing the birth of Jesus, who would bring peace and goodwill to the people. The Bible says we are to endeavor to be like Jesus, and "walk" as He did (more on that in chapter 10), so we, too, are to offer goodwill to others around us.

In Ephesians 6:7, Paul confirms this in his passage on how to work: "with goodwill doing service, as to the Lord, and not to men."

Goodwill means benevolent kindness, and you do that by being helpful, cooperative, and having empathy toward others. Think about each one of these words, and apply each to your day:

- *Friendly.* Be known as a person who is kind to others. Pleasant to be around. Interested in the lives of those around you. Sociable, amiable, caring, and gracious. I would suggest you know at least one personal thing about each coworker at our job and each neighbor. Something such as their hobby, children, or interesting relatives. Remember that about them, and bring it up in conversation on occasion. It will force you to be interested in them and become friendly.
- *Helpful.* Be reliable. Be observant of the needs of others, and willing to help. Being helpful puts the needs of others around you on your radar. Look for ways to be helpful, anticipate things that need to be done, and do them before being asked. Support what others are doing, be sympathetic to their struggles, and see if you can ease those struggles by simply offering a hand.
- *Cooperative.* Work with others to accomplish a goal. Do this joyfully, not begrudgingly.
- *Empathy.* Understand what someone needs and act on it, even if means just sitting with them for a while. The key word here is "understanding": that means you have to be somewhat close to them, and ask questions. Care about what others around you care about, at least enough to engage them. Jesus excelled at empathy. In any relationship, choosing empathy takes a conscious effort, but it usually produces great results. Not choosing empathy is easy, lazy, and possibly detrimental.

Having goodwill depends on having a good attitude and good feelings toward others. Sometimes you have to do a checkup from the neck up and improve your attitude. You may have to struggle to do that, but do it anyway. How? Paul tells us: "with goodwill doing service," linking those three words together (goodwill, doing, and service).

Goodwill is something you have to *do*. It takes effort and work. Paul assumes many of us have trouble being friendly, helpful, or outgoing enough to help others, so he says we have to work at it and make an intentional effort to *do* it. Find it hard? Do it anyway. It's your service, a service you provide.

One way to look at service is to think of it as a sort of duty to society, similar to military service. If that's hard, then compare it to servicing your car … something you have to do to keep it running. For example, engage your neighbor in a quick conversation every now and then. Eventually, you will serve others more often and more naturally.

When you look up the meaning of "service," it helps to understand this duty of a Christian, both in the noun form of the word and the verb. The noun form means "The action of helping or doing work for someone."[6] The verb means to "perform routine maintenance or repair work."[7]

If you still have trouble showing goodwill to others, Paul gives one additional end-all step to do goodwill: "as to the Lord, not to men."

Sometimes it just may be a seemingly impossible struggle to have and show goodwill toward someone. The Holy Spirit, through the writing of Paul, understands that may happen, so he says to look beyond any of your self-imposed obstacles: Look to the Lord Jesus Christ, and do goodwill as if you are doing it for Him.

Christians are often characterized as "negative averse." That's okay if your focus is on doing good works. You don't have to be bored and/or boring, where you are not light in the world and of little benefit to others or God. Instead, strive to be someone who is appreciated, respected, and revered. You don't have to engage others with unwholesome talk or deeds unbecoming of a Christian. Be above reproach, and avoid the appearance of evil as the Bible says so no one has anything bad to say about you. Be useful to God and to others.

Paul said this in 1 Thessalonians 4:11: "Aspire to lead a quiet life, to mind your own business, and to work with your own hands, as we commanded you." He was *not* saying "shut up and mind your own business, disconnect, and be a boring introverted wallflower." Quite the opposite, in fact.

In context, he was telling us to abstain from unwholesome talk, meddling, and gossiping—basically, not bothering ourselves with issues that don't concern us. In today's context, know when to just stay out of something. Don't be that person on Facebook that complains or ridicules or "shoots down" others.

The epitome of joy, fun, and excitement, emboldening the very spirit of "living life to the fullest" are Christians devoid of legalism, living fervently in spirit, zealous for doing good works, with fullness and confidence from the grace that is in Christ Jesus. (That's a long and deep sentence, I know, so read it again.)

So as to not exclude anyone, if you or others consider yourself rich, Paul talks to you about doing good in 1 Timothy 6:18: "[T]hose who are rich in this present age not to be haughty, nor to trust in uncertain riches but in the living God, who gives us richly all things to enjoy. Let them do good, that they be rich in good works, ready to give, willing to share, storing up for themselves a good foundation for the time to come, that they may lay hold on eternal life."

Do you like adventure?

Doing goodwill can become an adventure in your life. Look for ways to do good, even if you have to be creative and proactive. Consider it a fun thing to do each day. Make a task, even life itself, fun for others! Make doing good *your* thing. That's part of the "living life to the full" that Jesus said you would have through Him in John 10:10. It will bring Him glory when you do. And remembering Jesus when you do any good work is key.

Romans 12:11 and Titus 2:14 are good reminders and provide great encouragement. Look them up in your Bible from time to time.

It is comforting to know that God knows it's hard to do good and goodwill, and a person can get tired of that hard work. Galatians 6:9–10 and 1 Corinthians 15:58 tell us to not grow weary of going good. It will not go unnoticed and it isn't in vain. And you will reap a harvest "in due season" if you don't give up. That's a promise from God.

We live a full Christian life when we do God's good work to others.
—Helen Mitchell, Biola University

"For we are His workmanship, created in Christ Jesus for good works, which God prepared beforehand that we should walk in them" (Eph. 2:10).

PEOPLE CAN SPOT A FAKE

Do you greet someone with "Hi, how are you doing?" and walk away? If so, you are a disingenuous fake. I know that is just a saying, but it shouldn't be for a Christian. If you say "How are you?" you should look at the other person intently, waiting for an answer. Maybe you need to follow up with "No, really, how *are* you?" Just make sure you're ready for an answer and take the time to listen. That shows love and glorifies God.

When you ask people how they are, and you genuinely want to know, you are sending a clear message they are visible and have value. That shows love for others. You probably cannot read minds, so you may have to ask further questions such as "How is your job going," "Do you have plans for the weekend?" or "What's God doing in your life?" Here is a good one to ask: "Is there anything I can pray for you about?"

When I have asked someone that question, they always say yes … even if they are a non-Christian. And that's a great way connect with them … and maybe even share the gospel of Jesus. Be available for the Holy Spirit to use you to help or reach others.

Now even though most people reply "fine" to the question "How are you?" I have found that they rarely are. They typically have something in their life they really want to talk to somebody about! They need the love of others, and God has put you in front of them asking them "How are you?"

Now, give them some time to answer. Don't get all antsy as though you would rather be somewhere else. If people know you are too busy to hear them, they will assume they're of no value, and neither is anything you have to say to them. And while many have been credited with this saying, it certainly applies here: "People won't care how much you know until they know how much you care."

So have a demeanor about you that makes others feel *safe* around you:

- Remember, love starts by showing grace to others.
- Be welcoming and kind.
- Show you care by being generous with your time.
- Don't gossip about them to others.
- Show them you can be trusted with their issue(s).
- Always be transparent, with easy-going self-control.
- Don't be judgmental, or someone they have to gain approval from.
- Be genuine, and don't put on a false front.
- Assure them they don't have to put on a false front around you either.
- Be humble and peaceable.
- Offer your compassion or empathy.
- Be helpful, but not overbearing.
- Always approach the conversation with brotherly love.

Don't worry about what you will say, and don't use that as an excuse to avoid the conversation. The Holy Spirit will help you with that (Luke 12:12). Even if you can't come up with any eloquent words of wisdom, your love for others will shine through, simply by your caring enough to engage them. 1 Corinthians 1:17 says there is power in the good news of the gospel, not so much in eloquent words of wisdom.

As a suggestion, please do a word search in the Bible for the term "one another." You will find that love glorifies God when it is shown to others and becomes part of our daily walk.

Keep close to other Christians, and they will keep you close to Christ.

We love the spotlight, but God loves us in those moments where there's no light in us. May we love others as God does.
—Oswald Chambers

PRACTICAL APPLICATIONS

1. On a note card, write down a name of someone you could love more. Then write ways you can show that person love.

2. _____

   _____

3. _____

   _____

4 ABIDE

Jesus tells us a way to glorify God our Father in heaven is to bear much fruit. He said this during His incredible teaching on how to be a true Christian, and if you are, you bear fruit when you abide in Him and He in you. Here is what Jesus taught, and notice the keyword *abide* and how often He used it. Also notice what you get in return in verse 11:

John 15: 1–11

1. I am the true vine, and My Father is the vinedresser.
2. Every branch in Me that does not bear fruit He takes away; and every branch that bears fruit He prunes, that it may bear more fruit.
3. You are already clean because of the word which I have spoken to you.
4. Abide in Me, and I in you. As the branch cannot bear fruit of itself, unless it abides in the vine, neither can you, unless you abide in Me.
5. I am the vine, you are the branches. He who abides in Me, and I in him, bears much fruit; for without Me you can do nothing.
6. If anyone does not abide in Me, he is cast out as a branch and is withered; and they gather them and throw them into the fire, and they are burned.

7. If you abide in Me, and My words abide in you, you will ask what you desire, and it shall be done for you.
8. By this My Father is glorified, that you bear much fruit; so you will be My disciples.
9. As the Father loved Me, I also have loved you; abide in My love.
10. If you keep My commandments, you will abide in My love, just as I have kept My Father's commandments and abide in His love.
11. These things I have spoken to you, that My joy may remain in you, and that your joy may be full.

Consider all of these religious leaders who have followers: Jesus, Mohammed, Confucius, the Pope, the Dalai Lama, Joseph Smith, Buddha, and many more. Only one of them has fulfilled over three hundred prophesies. Only one of them was killed, came back to life—as witnessed by hundreds of people—and is still alive today. Only one is the one true God who came in the flesh so we can get to know Him, and made a way to be with God forever. Only one has paid the penalty in full for your sins, and only one loves you and wants to have a relationship with you. That "only one" is Jesus.

Jesus wants to help you have a fruitful joyous life, like grapes on a branch connected to a vine.

Bingo and wine

This idea of abiding in Him is one of those difficult-to-grasp concepts, but when you do, when the ideas line up and you understand this passage … well, the word "*Bingo!*" comes to mind. Jesus does a wonderful job of explaining "abiding in Him" using an analogy of a grapevine and branches. Wonderful products (such as wine and raisins) come from good grapes that are connected properly.

The main stalk or trunk of the grape plant is called a vine, and from it come branches with leaves, nonproducing withered stems, and stems that produce grapes. The vinedresser trims off the nonproducing stems, which can waste nutrients and bring disease to the branch and vine. Those are burned so as to not spread disease. (I'm sure you have already thought this *could* be a reference to hell… .)

The producing branches are propped up with a "helper," either a wooden support or wire the branches are tied to. I find it very interesting that in John 14:26, Jesus promised that a "Helper" would come to Christians: "A Helper, the Holy Spirit whom the Father will send in My name …" The Holy Spirit is called a Helper by Jesus and is a wonderful insight into how the Holy Spirit works to help us bear fruit by supporting us.

Jesus gave us a helpful clue to abiding well in John 8:31. He said, "If you abide in My word, you are My disciples indeed. And you shall know the truth, and the truth shall make you free."

The key to abiding in Jesus is Jesus. What I mean is this: John established in the first chapter of his book that Jesus is God's Word (John 1:1; 14). This is a difficult concept to grasp, but when you do and the light goes on, you will understand that only through the study of God's Word will you know Jesus and how to abide in Him, because Jesus and His Word, the Bible, is truth— truth that frees you to live an abundant life as Jesus Himself promised in John 10:10. Freedom and joy and abundance in this life comes when you abide in Jesus … seriously!

The branch of the vine does not worry, and toil, and rush here to seek for sunshine, and there to find rain. No; it rests in union and communion with the vine; and at the right time, and in the right way, is the right fruit found on it. Let us so abide in the Lord Jesus.
– James Hudson Taylor

JESUS GIVES THE RESULTS OF ABIDING.

Now, this word "abide" is used by Jesus often. It is key to bearing much fruit, so we need to carefully learn and act upon this word, which, as Jesus said in John 15:8, is how God is glorified.

- Abide is a verb—an action word. The original Greek word used here is pronounced *meno*, meaning to actively stay and to continue to be present in a place and to not depart. It means to live.
- "Abide in me." Remain united to Jesus through a living faith. Live a life of dependence on Jesus and obey His doctrines, imitate His example, and constantly exercise faith in Him. The word "remain"

is important. It means to persist or continue, especially after other similar or related things have ceased.

- "And I in you." If you truly abide in Jesus, He promises to "abide" in you, too.
- "Abide in me, and I in you." Jesus uses the analogy of a fruit tree branch to establish the basis of Christian living, a very deep and powerful analogy. To be brief, there are two kinds of branches: those that do not produce fruit and they are cut off and thrown into the fire, and those that produce fruit; all those are pruned, so they can produce even more fruit. Is pruning enjoyable for the branch? No, but through that hardship, comes more fruit.
- "Abide in me, and I in you." (Part two!) We can do nothing without Jesus. The branch cannot produce fruit itself; it must be attached to, and gain strength and nourishment from, the true vine, Jesus. We are a fruit-less branch destined for the fire if we are not abiding in and from Jesus!
- "If you abide in me, and My words abide in you." Do you know Scripture? Are you able to come up with a scriptural passage for most circumstances in life? Do you memorize Scripture? True believers obey Scripture and submit to it. If you are committed to His Word, you will be committed to His will. Therefore, your prayers will be fruitful, your life will be fruitful, and you will be a disciple of Jesus
- "Abide in My love." Jesus' love was both for His Father and for His people. When Jesus was asked what the greatest commandment was, He said it was to love God. The second was to love others. Love is a continued presence in a true believer, and Jesus provided the example we are to follow.
- "If you keep my commandments, you will abide in my love." Jesus said at other times, "If you love me, you will keep my command-ments." To love Jesus means 100 percent devotion to Him, His word, and His doctrines. If you do what He commands, you will abide in His love. Again, Jesus was the example or pattern we are to follow, which is why He said to abide in His love.
- Jesus spoke these things so His joy may remain in us, and that our joy will be full! Abiding correctly equals joy! Being joyful always comes from abiding in Him all ways!

ABIDE MEANS MORE THAN YOU THINK!

Here are several passages in Scripture where the word "abide" is found. Read each one and think about what abide means in each passage, because its meaning is a bit different in each one:

- Luke 24:29: "But they constrained Him, saying, 'Abide with us, for it is toward evening, and the day is far spent.' And He went in to stay with them."
- John 8:31: "Then Jesus said to those Jews who believed Him, "If you abide in My word, you are My disciples indeed."
- John 8:35: "And a slave does not abide in the house forever, but a son abides forever."
- John 12:46: "I have come as a light into the world, that whoever believes in Me should not abide in darkness."
- John 14:16: "And I will pray the Father, and He will give you another Helper, that He may abide with you forever—"
- John 15:4: "Abide in Me, and I in you. As the branch cannot bear fruit of itself, unless it abides in the vine, neither can you, unless you abide in Me."
- John 15:6: "If anyone does not abide in Me, he is cast out as a branch and is withered; and they gather them and throw them into the fire, and they are burned."
- John 15:7: "If you abide in Me, and My words abide in you, you will ask what you desire, and it shall be done for you."
- John 15:9: "As the Father loved Me, I also have loved you; abide in My love."
- John 15:10: "If you keep My commandments, you will abide in My love, just as I have kept My Father's commandments and abide in His love."
- 1 Corinthians 13:13: "And now abide faith, hope, love, these three; but the greatest of these *is* love."
- 1 John 2:24: "Therefore let that abide in you which you heard from the beginning. If what you heard from the beginning abides in you, you also will abide in the Son and in the Father."
- 1 John 2:27: "But the anointing which you have received from Him abides in you, and you do not need that anyone teach you; but as

the same anointing teaches you concerning all things, and is true, and is not a lie, and just as it has taught you, you will abide in Him."

- 1 John 2:28: "And now, little children, abide in Him, that when He appears, we may have confidence and not be ashamed before Him at His coming."
- 1 John 3:17: "But whoever has this world's goods, and sees his brother in need, and shuts up his heart from him, how does the love of God abide in him?"
- 1 John 4:13: "By this we know that we abide in Him, and He in us, because He has given us of His Spirit."
- 2 John 1:9: "Whoever transgresses and does not abide in the doctrine of Christ does not have God. He who abides in the doctrine of Christ has both the Father and the Son."

While working on this chapter, I kept typing the word "abode" when I meant *abide*. Do those things happen when you type, too? I sat back, frustrated at myself after doing that for the "umpteenth" time, before I realized, the words are very similar. Do you abide (live) in the abode (home) of Jesus? When you describe where you live, does it include Jesus? Think about that.

PRACTICAL APPLICATION

How will we know if we're abiding in Jesus, not something or someone else, such as abiding in ourselves? Good question, huh?! Instead of writing down some practical applications as in other chapters, this section is different. I looked for an example, or steps to follow, which is the best way to apply this critical way of glorifying God.

The answer showed up when reading one of the psalms for a morning devotion one day. How fitting that the criteria I can use to "judge" my abiding in Jesus aptitude is found in the Old Testament. We live in the age of grace, since Jesus came to fulfill the Old Testament laws. The Old Testament points to Jesus. Jesus quoted a lot from the Old Testament and especially the psalms. Often, in fact, He is the fulfillment of many of the psalms.

So it made sense to me to use Psalm 15 as a "measuring tape" to see how I am doing abiding in Jesus, and I found eleven character traits as the "marks on the tape measure":

ELEVEN CHARACTER TRAITS OF THOSE WHO ABIDE WITH GOD

Psalm 15

"LORD, who may abide in Your tabernacle? Who may dwell in Your holy hill?"

(I hang out with God. I enjoy being with Him and going to church.)

1. "He who walks uprightly,"
   (I abide when I focus on God and seek Him most, and follow His principles.)
2. "And works righteousness,"
   (I abide when I *do* works that are right, noble, honest, true, and of good report.)
3. "And speaks the truth in his heart";
   ("Out of the heart, the mouth speaks": I abide when I have God's truth in my heart, and speak it often.)
4. "He who does not backbite with his tongue,"
   (When I don't talk about people, even behind their back, I am abiding in Jesus.)
5. "Nor does evil to his neighbor,"
   (I abide when I show love to others and don't do any bad things to them.)
6. "Nor does he take up a reproach against his friend; (In whose eyes a vile person is despised ...)"
   (I abide in Jesus when I don't criticize my friends, but I stand by them, like Jesus.)
7. "But he honors those who fear the LORD";
   (I abide when I hold up in high esteem people who emulate Jesus well.)
8. "He who swears to his own hurt and does not change";
   (Abiding in Jesus means I keep my word, even if it's hard or hurts. It means keeping a "steady, even keel.")
9. "He who does not put out his money at usury,"
   (Abiding in Jesus means I don't take advantage of others and don't

profit from them unfairly, including doing things for others with the intent of getting something in return.)
10. "Nor does he take a bribe against the innocent."
    (I don't make myself look good by making others look bad. I also don't persuade others to sin or do something I wouldn't do.)
11. "He who does these things shall never be moved."
    (When I abide in Jesus, I am rock solid, not shaken by events around me or circumstances that may affect me. I hold fast to Jesus, doing these things because they are like an anchor keeps a boat steady in stormy seas.)

There is one more trait of those who abide in Jesus: it's having a helper. Jesus Himself said when we abide in Him, He will send a Helper: the Holy Spirit. Those who abide in Him have the Holy Spirit. The apostle John heard this and got very excited about it when he considered Jesus' statement that He would be with us always. Jesus abides in us when we abide in Him. He wrote about it in 1 John 3:24, where he ended a very powerful chapter on how to live the Christian life: "Now he who keeps His commandments abides in Him, and He in him. And by this we know that He abides in us, by the Spirit whom He has given us."

John's writings in the book of 1 John expand on the theme of the commonality we Christians have in Jesus. John harkens back to when he heard Jesus teach and reflects on a practical way of knowing if we are abiding in Jesus ... and Jesus in us through the Holy Spirit. He tells is this very tangible and practical way of knowing how well we are abiding in Him in John 13:35 where he quotes Jesus: "By this all will know that you are My disciples, if you have love for one another."

Remember, without a love of others, your abiding in Jesus is basically worthless, at least to others whom you are to be salt and light. Paul said in 1 Corinthians 12:1 that without love, what you say is just annoying fruitless noise like clanging cymbals or sounding brass.

Abiding in Jesus produces love for others that is genuine and they relate to.

BE FRUITFUL AND MULTIPLY IS THE FIRST COMMAND.

In the first chapter in the Bible, God gave the first command. It's to be fruitful and multiply. To the plants He gave that command in Genesis 1:11; to the animals, fish, and birds, He commanded them to be fruitful and multiply in verse 22. Then He created man and woman in verse 27 and said: "Then God blessed them, and God said to them, 'Be fruitful and multiply; fill the earth and subdue it'" (Gen. 1:28).

Many people think that command was to have babies, but it is so much more! We are to be creative and improve our surroundings for the betterment of ourselves and other people God loves. God "wired" each of us with gifts and abilities to carry out that command and expects us to obey that command. If you are a true Christian, this also means to use what God has given you to be productive spiritually as well, enhancing the lives of others ... serving Jesus.

Jesus taught this command to be fruitful and multiply on several occasions, hammering home how important that command is in no uncertain terms. In the parable of the talents in Matthew 25:14–29, the man gave each person a "talent" and expected them to be fruitful and multiply. Those who did were given an eternal life reward, and the person that didn't was sent to a very bad place of weeping and gnashing of teeth.

Another instance was when Jesus walked by a fig tree in Matthew 21:18–19. He wanted some of the fruit from the tree. Unfortunately, it didn't produce any, so Jesus cursed the tree, and it withered away immediately.

This is *very* serious. Jesus expects us to be fruitful and multiply to enhance this world for Him! Are you? Are you more fruitful now than a few years ago? How about a year from now?

WHAT ARE OUR FRUITS?

What are the fruits we are to produce? Are we to be fruitful? What does that even *mean*?

I'm so glad you asked! I found two people in the Bible I admire and thought would have great advice. The first is Paul, who was a wonderful teacher, so he must say what fruit is, and I didn't have to look far to find his answer in Galatians 5:22–23: "But the fruit of the Spirit is love, joy, peace, longsuffering, kindness, goodness, faithfulness, gentleness, self-control."

Absolutely perfect and succinct, right? Paul nailed it with just nine words. I could expand on each one, but since Paul didn't, assuming we are all smart enough to figure out what they mean, I will leave it right there. These are all things we do, by the way, or are produced when we are connected to the Vine (Jesus). No connection, no nine fruits. They are attitudes and character traits. And here is the thing … when we are fruitful the result is "and multiply." Think about that: How would being kind to someone and doing right by them, for instance, multiply kindness and goodness? It spreads exponentially, as that person does the same for others too. See what I mean?!

So, then, the other guy is Peter, whom I thought would tell us, since he is a regular, hard-working guy like each one of us in so many ways. He probably learned what fruit is, heard Jesus teach about it, and would know the practical application in our life. I looked and looked … and was very surprised to find this perfect elaboration on how to be fruitful in very practical ways in 2 Peter 1: 5–11:

> But also for this very reason, giving all diligence, add to your faith virtue, to virtue knowledge, to knowledge self-control, to self-control perseverance, to perseverance godliness, to godliness brotherly kindness, and to brotherly kindness love.
>
> For if these things are yours and abound, you will be neither barren nor unfruitful in the knowledge of our Lord Jesus Christ. For he who lacks these things is shortsighted, even to blindness, and has forgotten that he was cleansed from his old sins. Therefore, brethren, be even more diligent to make your call and election sure, for if you do these things you will never stumble; for so an entrance will be supplied to you abundantly into the everlasting kingdom of our Lord and Savior Jesus Christ.

Virtue literally means "the God-given ability to perform heroic deeds." It also means "excellence" and "praiseworthy." In his reference to good deeds, which causes someone to say "praise God for you!" Peter is writing of moral energy, the God-based power to perform deeds of excellence.

Knowledge is knowing what's in the Bible. It's the ability to correctly discern truth from error, right from wrong, and good from evil. Discernment is lacking in our Christian culture but is commanded of us in countless locations in Scripture. This includes holding on to and voicing truth as well as exposing untruth. This can only come with diligent daily study of the Word of God and the help of the Holy Spirit.

Self-control literally means "holding oneself." Keeping an even keel. Being self-restrained and self-disciplined. Keeping our emotions even and our thoughts and responses predictive and based on the Word of God. We are to not allow outside occurrences to dictate how we act. We are also to let our mind control our emotions, not the other way around. We are to make sure Christ is seen in us and our words and our actions.

Perseverance means patience with endurance in doing what is right, never giving in to temptation or trial. We have perseverance when we have God-given abilities to perform, knowledge of what is right, self-control and "staying power," an attitude of not quitting, and an absolute and vibrant hope. It all boils down to having hope and trust in God, His sovereignty, His power, and His future promises to us.

Godliness means to live in reverence, loyalty, and obedience to God. God gives us every resource to be godly. We just need to use those resources faithfully. We need to be more like Jesus. For us, "godly" does not mean perfect, but faithfully obedient. Jesus said in John 15 without Him, we can do nothing, and with Him, we will be fruitful (and therefore have godliness).

Brotherly kindness love means putting the above into practice ... putting legs on the above words. By putting others before ourselves, we do acts of kindness, show genuine concern and care, and show the love of Jesus through us, being the physical manifestation of God's loving will. Notice the term has no punctuation: "brotherly kindness love." The three words are connected; they go together, as if one word or concept. As Peter says in his previous book, "And above all things have fervent love for one another for love will cover over a multitude of sins."

Notice the progression of these fruits. One builds on the previous. Are you progressing?

Trees are always growing and producing more fruit each season. We should always be growing in biblical knowledge and maturity in Christ. Have you grown in the past year? Are you producing more fruit now than a few years ago?

Dozens of passages in the Bible tell us to be fruitful, and most of them are composed of the words of Jesus. Are you obeying His words? We are not saved by our fruit, but the fruit is evidence of being saved because fruitfulness is not what we do for God, it is what God does through us. We do, however, have to initiate the fruitfulness … we have to create the opportunity for God to work through us. Are you being proactive looking for ways to be fruitful, or reactive, waiting for ways to come to you? Being proactive is always best.

Notice Peter said we do not have a spirit of fear or timidity, but of power, love, and self-control. If we do not have the spirit of those three attributes, then we need to ask ourselves what spirit *do* we have?! Peter implies in his passage that maturing as a Christian is evidenced by a spirit of power, love, and self-discipline.

Oh, and notice Peter also says if you do these things, you will never stumble, which is similar to the ending of Psalm 15 where David said we will never be moved. Stumbling makes us look bad, and it *hurts*.

HOW DO I KNOW IF I AM BEING FRUITFUL?

Check and see if you are doing these in your day-to-day life: Being thankful and giving praise in front of others and being content (Heb. 13:5), ministering to other believers (Rom. 1:13), living righteously (Rom. 6:22), giving money (Rom. 15:23 & Phil. 4:17), sowing or reaping (John 4).

Live a life characterized with joy and hope in such a way such that people not only notice, they ask you about it (1 Peter 3:51). That is when being becomes doing. Being like Jesus (2 Cor. 2:15), which pours out of you so that your life is different than most other people, and they notice and want to be like that.

When Jesus said abiding in Him will produce fruit and that producing fruit glorifies God, we need to pay attention. We need to do it if we call ourselves Christians. We need to obey Him.

However strong the branch becomes, however far away it reaches round the home, out of sight of the vine, all its beauty and all its fruitfulness ever depend upon that one point of contact where it grows out of the vine. So be it with us too.
—Andrew Murray, *Holy in Christ*

5   OBEDIENCE

Obedience to Him is something you do: It started when you obeyed Jesus' call to "follow me," and continues in your personal life and your influence on those around you. It's a show of patience, love, and devotion to Him and demonstrates your faith and trust in Him. It also glorifies God. God wants you to obey Him. He knows what's best for you—it's all about that—so don't add to it.

A few of us have a favorite chapter in the Bible. Most of us have several favorites, so we're hard pressed to pick just one. I probably can't pick one as my favorite, so let's just say I have a "Top 10."

John 14 is among them. We learn so much about Jesus and living the Christian life from this chapter where He held a "question and answer" session with His guys. Obedience to Him seemed to come up often, and it's probably the underlying theme. In fact, right smack dab in the middle is verse 15, which fittingly becomes the central theme: Jesus said, "If you love Me, keep My commandments."

THE BIBLICAL CONCEPT OF OBEDIENCE

To get this concept of obedience firmly planted in our mind, here are a few (okay … more than a few) scriptural passages.[8] Personally, I like to look for a keyword that "jumps out" to make them come alive:

- "Love the LORD your God and keep his requirements, his decrees, his laws and his commands always" (Deut. 11:1 NIV).

   The key word I see here is *always*. We are to love God and obey Him always.

- "We demolish arguments and every pretension that sets itself up against the knowledge of God, and we take captive every thought to make it obedient to Christ" (2 Cor. 10:5).

   The phrase *"take captive every thought"* jumps out here, since everything starts with a thought. That turns into an attitude, then to an action. So capture your every thought and make it obedient to God.

- "This calls for patient endurance on the part of the people of God who keep his commands and remain faithful to Jesus" (Rev. 14:12).

   "Patient endurance" is key here. Couple that with the words "faithful to Jesus," and you have what it takes to keep His commands.

- "Through him we received grace and apostleship to call all the Gentiles to the obedience that comes from faith for his name's sake" (Rom. 1:5).

   Faith is the key in this passage. It takes faith to be obedient … remember our previous topic of faith? It is impossible to please God without it.

   There is one other key phrase here: "for his name's sake." To me, that means when you were saved, you took on the name "Christian." So being obedient to Christ will make sure you live up to that name.

- "Have confidence in your leaders and submit to their authority, because they keep watch over you as those who must give an account. Do this so that their work will be a joy, not a burden, for that would be of no benefit to you" (Heb. 13:17).

Confidence is the key word here—confidence in the leaders God has placed over you and certainly confidence in the things God expects you to be obedient to.

- "If you love me, keep my commands" (John 14:15).

    Love is the key word here. You keep Jesus' commands because of your love for Him.

- "You are my friends if you do what I command" (John 15:14).

    Are you a *friend* of Jesus? You are when you keep His commands.

- "And this is love: that we walk in obedience to his commands. As you have heard from the beginning, his command is that you walk in love" (2 John 1:6).

    Walk is mentioned twice here. It means obedience is something you have to actively do … like walking. You walk because you intend to go somewhere. Intentionally obey Jesus because of love, which takes some effort and direction.

- "The Israelites had moved about in the wilderness for forty years until all the men who were of military age when they left Egypt had died, since they had not obeyed the LORD. For the LORD had sworn to them that they would not see the land he had solemnly promised their ancestors to give us, a land flowing with milk and honey" (Josh. 5:6).

    Promised is what strikes me here. Not obeying God caused them to miss the promises of God.

- "God 'will repay each person according to what they have done.' To those who by persistence in doing good seek glory, honor and immortality, he will give eternal life. But for those who are self-seeking and who reject the truth and follow evil, there will be wrath and anger" (Rom. 2:6–8).

    Repay is the key word here. If you are persistent in obeying Him, God will repay you (maybe here or maybe in heaven) according to what you have done for God, for His glory, for His honor, and for your eternal life in heaven. But if you are self-seeking and reject His truth, you will get His wrath and anger.

- "He replied, 'Blessed rather are those who hear the word of God and obey it'" (Luke 11:28).

Blessed is what I want to be. Jesus said you would be blessed if you hear and obey God's Word.

- "As obedient children, do not conform to the evil desires you had when you lived in ignorance" (1 Pet. 1:14).

  Do not conform seems to be the key phrase here. Conform to God's Word now that you are a true Christian, not to the evil desires you used to indulge in.

- "But whoever looks intently into the perfect law that gives freedom, and continues in it—not forgetting what they have heard, but doing it—they will be blessed in what they do" (James 1:25).

  This one is jam-packed with keywords: Look *intently* into God's Word—it gives *freedom. Continue* in it, don't *forget* it, and *do* it. You will be *blessed* when you *do.*

"IS OBEDIENCE REALLY THAT IMPORTANT?"

When Israel was obedient to God, her people flourished. When they did not obey, they became sickly and were overtaken by their enemies. We Christians are also blessed and glorify God when we live within the big "O" of obedience, and when we stray outside that "O," we get into trouble, and God is not glorified. It's that simple.

Being obedient means we *serve* Him. Several New Testament writers started out by calling themselves "Bondservants of Christ," which means a loyal servant ("slave" is the actual word) of Jesus Christ who has chosen willingly to serve Him. Good servants who bring honor and glory to their master are obedient, productive, and fruitful.

In numerous passages throughout the Bible (John 15 is one), we are commanded to bear fruit. We are to be productive, and our "produce" is obedience, love, attitude, and good deeds. In John 15, you will notice some fruitful things we are *told* to do by God, and some are things we *just do for Him* and His kingdom.

Obedience happens when we do the things we are commanded to in Scripture. We're *fruitful* when we do the things that serve Him and enhance His kingdom. Those actions start in our *heart,* our innermost part, then grow and blossom from there into our *attitude,* which produces the fruit that is our *deeds*. When those are pleasing to God according to His Word, He is then glorified.

"By this My Father is glorified, that you bear much fruit; so you will be My disciples" (John 15:8).

"Keep your heart with all diligence, for out of it spring the issues of life" (Prov. 4:23).

"The righteous shall be glad in the LORD, and trust in Him. And all the upright in heart shall glory" (Ps. 64:10).

Wouldn't it be wonderful if your responses to the issues of your life are glorifying to God? It starts in your heart and comes from being obedient to Him and His Word.

OBEDIENCE HAS TO BE LEARNED.

How do we learn to be obedient? By reading God's Word and hearing by attending church services or a small group Bible, studying and listening to Christian podcasts, and taking part in Christian living seminars, workshops, or conferences. We strengthen our obedience through listening to sermons from some of our favorite pastors and reading the Bible regularly. What to read? John is really good … read *that* book. Then read Ephesians because the first three chapters explain our boundaries, and the next three chapters tell us how to live in those boundaries. Then read other "how-to books" such as 1 John, James, then Philippians, then …

How did you learn to drive in an obedient manner? You studied the driver's manual, and you took driver's ed. Similarly, read the Christian's manual (the Bible) and take Christian Ed (going to church, absorbing sermons and podcasts, and attending Sunday school classes and Christian workshops).

When you read those "how to live obediently" passages in the Bible, you will discover that the boundaries God has placed for you are for your own safety and betterment. You will also discover there's immense freedom inside that boundary, freedom that is full of joy, peace, and contentment.

"Obedience sounds limiting ... little freedom and no fun, right?"

G. K. Chesterton tells a story (and this is my paraphrase here) of a town in England that built a very nice park and playground for the children of the town. Swings, jungle gyms, slides, and so on were thoughtfully spaced around the park. However, the kids only seemed to congregate in the center of the park and played only on the merry-go-round in the middle. No one played on any of the much better equipment near the edges of the park.

Someone suggested a fence be put around the perimeter of the park with just two gates. When the city installed the fence, the kids came to play and, to everyone's amazement, the kids scattered all over the park, laughing and playing, enjoying all the equipment ... even up to the very edges of the fence line.

See, boundaries give joyous and abundant freedom. As Jesus said in John 10:10, His boundaries gives life ... more *abundant* life. Many of you have been to a place such as the Grand Canyon, where we are afraid to get close to the edge and look over, but when there is a steel rail barrier, we get right up to it and lean over, taking in the full view of God's majestic creation. There is peace in boundaries.

I like to call it "Living within the Big 'O' of Obedience." It's as though God has placed a huge fence around your life, defining where that fence is, and when you live inside that fence, life is wonderful and full of blessings. When you wander outside that fence, life gets hard, and there are minimal blessings. Usually, what's outside the fence looks good and fun and inviting, but we've all learned the hard way that the grass isn't always greener on the other side; it's greenest where you are supposed to be, where you water and fertilize. Live inside the "Big O."

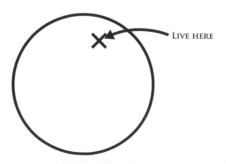

I'm sure you already know this, but the fence, or boundary, is made up of commandments such as "don't lie," "don't steal," "abstain from sex before marriage," "don't commit adultery," "love others as yourself," "honor your father and mother," "don't drink and drive," and so on. Each of which is actually for your own good. God is not a cosmic killjoy, but a loving Father who is trying to protect you and others from harm so you can enjoy life to the fullest.

The only people who get upset about you setting boundaries are the ones who were benefiting from you having none.
—Toby McKeehan (TobyMac)

Here is what Moses told God's people in Deuteronomy 6:7–9 about the Law they had at the time, the Ten Commandments. Can you find four specific things to do here?

"You shall teach them diligently to your children, and shall talk of them when you sit in your house, when you walk by the way, when you lie down, and when you rise up. You shall bind them as a sign on your hand, and they shall be as frontlets between your eyes. You shall write them on the doorposts of your house and on your gates" (NKJV).

Teach God's requirements to your kids, talk about them with others all day long, know them like the back of your hand (as they should be the first thing that pops into your mind), and hang a few signs of God's words around your house and on your refrigerator.

Being obedient involves many things: trusting God, being patient, and loving others all come to mind. In fact, being patient with others and loving them are mentioned as ways to glorify God because those are traits of God as well: "Now may the God of patience and comfort grant you to be like-minded toward one another, according to Christ Jesus, that you may with one mind and one mouth glorify the God and Father of our Lord Jesus Christ" (Rom. 15:5–6).

THE CHRISTIAN TIRE

I am reminded of a picture of a wheel representing your Christian life, where Jesus is at the center of the wheel, and the four spokes are the four components of your Christian life: reading the Bible, prayer, fellowship with believers, and witnessing to unbelievers. And the rubber portion of the wheel that meets the road is your Christian life in action.

Tires have the manufacturer's name on the sidewall as well as the brand name of the tire and what the tire is to be used for, such as snow, rain, or heavy loads. The tread is important, too, able to handle hazards and move away rainwater and snow to ensure good contact with the road.

You are like a tire. Yours should say "God's," "Christian," and "Used for His Service." Remember that analogy whenever you see tires and ask yourself, "Does my life have God's and Christian where others can 'see'? Am I doing what God 'designed' me to do?"

Think about that analogy some more. Look at the sketch above. You are so much like a tire, it's amazing (I'm being serious here), and you are smart enough to equate these features to your life:

- Jesus is the center of the wheel and enables God's power (the engine) to get to the tread and move the vehicle.
- Four spokes are required to transfer power to the tread:
- Bible reading. This is the main spoke, but it does not work without the other three.
- Prayer. Communicating with God goes with reading the Bible. That's two-way communication, which sets your focus where it belongs and transfers power.

- Fellowship. We gain strength from God through Jesus and other Christians who encourage us, keep us accountable, help us, and teach us (as we do with others too).
- Witnessing. At least make sure others see the hope of Christ in us gives us purpose and focus, which includes having a ready answer for those who ask about the hope in us.

All of these go together to make a well-rounded (pun intended) Christian, able to do as God (the engine) intends. Where the rubber meets the road is how all this comes together and moves the car forward ... your life and your impact on society. It's how you glorify God.

The tread on the tires (your outward life) is very effective at handling road hazards, such as siphoning away rainwater to maintain traction for the car, plowing through snow, and digging through mud. Rocks are hard and sharp, but they don't affect the car at all as the tires pop them out of the way or go right over them with no effort or consequence. Tires pay real close attention when the road is icy, looking for the best traction, while still getting the car down the road.

Air pressure (Holy Spirit) in the tire is very important. If not enough, the tire struggles to move the car, no matter how much power is applied, and if there's no pressure at all, the car stops completely. Air cannot be seen but is vital to helping the tire do its job. The tire doesn't pay much attention to the air it cannot see but relies heavily on it nonetheless. The air actually helps transfer power from the engine to the tread of the tire, but few recognize its importance until it's gone.

As with any car, work truck, or especially a race car, people don't talk much about the tires. All the discussion is about the engine (God) and its horsepower, torque, fuel mileage, and so on. The best tires like it that way ... they just want the car to win the race or deliver the passengers safely.

Another thing to notice is that tires really don't care about the stereo, the seats, the headlights, and so on. They don't let any of those affect their performance. Their purpose is to transfer power from the engine to the road and move the car forward. Tires are not concerned with what the seats have to say; they don't even care what color the car is. All tires appropriately think they are propelling a fire-red 790 horsepower Ferrari, or a 3,500HD chipped Duramax[9] truck.

Be like that—be a Christian tire.

"SO WHAT IS THE PURPOSE OF ME BEING OBEDIENT?"

Let me answer that with another question: What purpose does God have you fulfilling now in your day job, in your home job (as a spouse or parent), and what you volunteer to do or give? If you cannot provide specifics to all of those, you are probably not obedient to God's purpose or purposes. Just like the tire analogy, rely on God's power through Jesus, use fully the four "spokes" of Christian life, rely on the help of the Holy Spirit, deal with the hazards life throws at you, and get the job done.

Don't be concerned with things that have little or no effect on you such as other people, what your TV is like, or the color or location of your home. Just do your job glorifying God. Jesus didn't spend much effort trying to please other people or worrying about what he wore or what people thought about Him when it came to biblical things. He spent more effort obeying God and getting the job done.

We are also obedient when we trust God and let Him handle justice when it really is beyond our means to do so. I am reminded of Leviticus 10:1 3, where Aaron's two sons did something profane and disobedient, and "fire went out from the LORD and devoured them." Then God said, "By those who come near Me I must be regarded as holy; And before all the people I must be glorified." Those guys were adults, outside of Aaron's influence, so Aaron held his peace and let God handle justice.

When you seek to glorify yourself for something God deserves the glory for, you are on very treacherous ground. Stay off of that self-centered ground and get over to God-centered ground where you glorify God obediently. An extreme case of someone who did not glorify God but let others tell him he was God or like God was Herod, whose lack of glorifying God resulted in a very violent death. You can read about it in Acts 12:20–24.

Those things may not happen to us, thanks to Jesus, but it's important to learn from those passages how serious it is to obediently glorify God, not ourselves, and I will say this: regard God as holy, obey Him as best as you can, give Him credit when due, and endeavor to glorify Him.

"SOUNDS HARD."

Before we wind down this way to glorify God, to be obedient to His Word, the Bible, and to His commands, I want to look at the last command Jesus gave us in Matthew 28:18–19: "All authority has been given to Me in heaven and on earth. Go therefore and make disciples of all the nations, baptizing them in the name of the Father and of the Son and of the Holy Spirit, teaching them to observe all things that I have commanded you; and lo, I am with you always, even to the end of the age."

Jesus said He has been given all authority in heaven and earth. He is the highest authority there is or ever will be ... period. So think about this: If your boss told you to do something, you would. If the governor did, you would obey him even more. How about if the president of the United States commanded you to do something? You most certainly would execute his or her wishes, immediately and flawlessly! So when Jesus, who has way more authority than those leaders, tells you to do something, how awesome would it be to, first of all, get a command from Him and, second, endeavor to do it in a heartbeat and with your most serious focus and attention?

Now, one command you must obey from the Ruler of the Universe is to make disciples ... and to teach them to observe (obey) all things He said. If you've been a true Christian for at least a little while, do you have disciples you are mentoring? You'd better ... the Ruler of the Universe commanded you to.Jesus gave a pattern for you to follow, too. He had three disciples He worked really closely with, Peter, James, and John; then he had the other nine He mentored, which made up the twelve disciples. Scripture tells us he also had an additional seventy people He mentored and taught to spread His gospel. And then there were the "masses" He influenced, so:

$$\text{You} \rightarrow 3 \rightarrow 12 \rightarrow 70 \rightarrow \text{masses.}$$

It might sound overwhelming, but get to work on three "disciples" to mentor, or at least start with one. Who knows, if those three also mentor three, and they, in turn, mentor three … there could be masses from you! (More on this in the "Teach" chapter).

I think another pattern in Scripture is to be *mentored by* someone and *to mentor* someone. Jesus commanded us to mentor someone … so start with one and work up to three people you can make "disciples" of Jesus. You will be obedient to Him then, and that will bring glory to God.

You have help. Yes, when Jesus left the earth, He said He would send a Helper (the Holy Spirit), whom we talked about in chapter 4. It also takes effort from you to obey. It seems to always take extra effort and conscious strength to obey God, which glorifies Him as Isaiah 25:3 indicates: "Therefore, the strong people will glorify You; The city of the terrible nations will fear You."

"RELIGIONS THAT FORCE US TO OBEY BOTHER ME."

They bother me too, and they really bothered Jesus. Jesus was the most anti-religion person to ever live. People today just don't realize that. In Matthew 23 Jesus got so frustrated with the religious leaders when he was on the earth, with their rules and unhealthy requirements. Obeying Jesus should be because we want to, because we know it's the best way to live, because Jesus wants us to, not because we are forced to.

Religion says "I obey therefore I am accepted by God." The Gospel says "I am accepted by God through Christ, therefore I obey."
—Tim Keller

"WHY SHOULD I BE OBEDIENT? WHAT DO I GET?"

We have been so conditioned to the concept of doing something only for a reward, we automatically think, "What do I get when I'm, like, obedient?" Well, the reward will blow you away … and it's such an awesome reward, it will last forever. In a word, it's *joy*. Look to Jesus, who was obedient to God even until death … a horrible death on a cross, who for the joy endured that horrific suffering on the cross. "Wait, did you say Jesus had joy when He was crucified?" No, I did not, but Jesus allowed Himself to be put through that for us. He did so obediently because when it was over, there was joy for Him for doing so.

Wouldn't you agree that eternal joy is worth the hardships in our earthly life in the name of obedience? And, what hardships does being obedient to Jesus, put you through...really?

Here is another reward: The obedient Christian is obedient because of the salvation we have from Jesus along with our *love for Him*, and the reward is spending eternity with Him in heaven. "Eye has not seen, nor ear heard, nor have entered into the heart of man the things which God has prepared for those who love him." This promise from God is found in 1 Corinthians 2:9.

OBEDIENCE IN MARRIAGE IS FANTASTIC!

When each spouse obeys God's pattern in marriage, the result is a healthy, fulfilling, and rewarding marriage and family life. When each spouse is obedient to the brilliantly designed roles God has for each, their marriage is absolutely fantastic! It's a continual process, but it's definitely worth the effort. Similarly, when children are obedient to what God asks of them, they have a fun childhood and grow up trained for a wonderful and long life. Here are just a quick overview of the roles of each spouse as outlined in God's Word:

- Husbands are given the role of leader of the family (Eph. 5:23), especially as the spiritual leader. Think of two equal cars taking a two-lane exit off of the freeway side by side. Then those lanes merge into one lane just before the stop sign. One has to yield to the other, or they will crash. Similarly, in marriage, where the wife and husband are equal, there will be times when God says that to avoid a crash, the husband is the one to move to the lead. To minimize the effects on the other car (wife) the husband is told to:
  - Love her. For various reasons, your job is to show your wife love, in a way she understands. Men generally are stronger and can be more verbally abusive than women are, so to keep those traits at bay. Remember, God says to *love* your wife. According to Colossians 3:19, everything you say or do should be out of love, or you shouldn't do (or say) it at all. Few men understand

this, but your wife longs to feel loved. It makes her happy. And she probably needs to be reminded she is loved every day.

- ○ Dwell with her: Make a home with here where she is safe and comfortable and able to talk openly, and where she trusts you 100 percent. Just as you need her, she fills in your shortcomings. You remain constantly faithful as 1 Peter 3:7 says.

- Love her with understanding. Get your doctoral degree in your wife. Learn all about your wife, what she likes, doesn't like, and how she wants you to show her love and appreciation, and so on. This takes time, but God says to spend the time.

  - ○ Wives are to be submissive in those times. A wife needs to let her husband lead. As a wife, you have equal say, but in the end, when a decision has to be made, let him make it. Being submissive doesn't mean you take any abuse, or are second class in any way; it simply means you "let his car move ahead when the road narrows to one lane." God placed him in charge, he answers to God (who is just), so let him lead. He loves you, so let him show it in his leadership too (Col. 3:18).

  - ○ Respect your husband. Few women understand this, but a guy longs to be respected. It makes him happy. He probably needs to feel respect from you every day (Eph. 5:33).

  - ○ You respect him by supporting him, making him feel like the king of your home. When you do that, he'll more than likely do a great job. So let him lead. Don't second-guess, don't nag, and don't ridicule. Remain constantly faithful (Prov. 21:9; 31:10–12).

  - ○ You help him and complete him. He needs help. He needs *you*, as you have traits and abilities he does not. They complement the good traits he does have (Gen. 2:18–24).

When a marriage is based on obedience to God's Word

- A wife feels loved, appreciated, fulfilled, taken care of, joyous, full of purpose, equally important, and satisfied with her marriage. She will look forward to being with her husband after work. She puts effort into her marriage. She glorifies God.

- A husband feels respected, fulfilled, appreciated, loved, joyous, at peace, obedient to God, and satisfied. He is blessed. He looks forward to coming home to be with his wife. He glorifies God and honors Him because he continually works on his marriage and sees it improve over time.

WELL DONE, GOOD AND FAITHFUL ...

And there are more reasons to be obedient: Hearing Jesus say to you, "Well done good and faithful servant, enter into the joy of your Lord," should be a goal ... and reason to be obedient.

When you get to heaven, you want to hear this from Jesus, which hopefully, for you, is enough of a reward in itself for all your years and efforts serving Him obediently:

- *Well*—You did well with your life here on earth, obedient to His commands and callings.
- *Done*—You obediently finished what He entrusted you to do.
- *Good*—You "did good" at what He gave you to do, you were good to others, and did good things.
- *Faithful*—You remained faithful to Him, even in hardships, and kept the faith even to the end.
- *Servant*—You had an obedient servant's heart. You served Him, and you served others.
- *Enter into the joy of your Lord*—Jesus is filled with joy over your obedience ... forever!

Does your life story glorify God? If not so far, then start a new chapter now! Make it an intentional priority to do things not as much for yourself, but more things for the glory of God!

Don't shine so others can see you. Shine so that through you others can see Him!
—C. S. Lewis

PRACTICAL APPLICATIONS

1. Self-discipline is used to be obedient. How can you develop more self-discipline? Practice. Pick something to do for someone else and do it regularly. (Make the bed, do the dishes, make coffee, or... .)

2. _____

_____

3. _____

_____

6 ACKNOWLEDGE (HIM)

Proverbs 3:5–7 should be memorized by every Christian. Verse 6 says if we *acknowledge* Him in everything we do, He will direct our paths. The word "path" or "paths" is mentioned over sixty-five times in the Bible, and nearly all of them have something to do with God making your path in life a little smoother, a little straighter, or Him guiding your path if you let Him for your good and His glory. It means your path will be purposeful. But we have to acknowledge Him when walking life's paths.

"Trust in the LORD with all your heart, And lean not on your own understanding; In all your ways acknowledge Him, And He shall direct your paths" (Prov. 3:5–6).

Teach me, my God and King, in all things thee to see.
—George Herbert (The Elixir)

"WHAT DOES THIS WORD 'ACKNOWLEDGE' MEAN?"

First, *acknowledge* means to recognize the authority of someone or to agree with someone. When we are genuinely obligatory to God and let Him be the authority of what we do, then our path in life is smoother and straighter. Psalm 16:11 says, "You make known to me the path of life." So your best path shouldn't be a secret or elusive. If you acknowledge Him, you will be on the best path. It may be hilly, windy, rocky, and rainy along the path at times, but usually those times seem harder on you when you focus on the path instead of God. God can, however, use those tough times on the path to make you stronger and more trusting of Him for better paths in the future.

But still, during those harsh times, that path can actually be smoother and straighter when we acknowledge God as we walk it. It involves trusting Him, obeying Him, and thanking Him, but acknowledging Him always comes first.

When we are on *our* path of *our* ideas, *our* wishes, *our* understanding, and *our* plan, we get the glory, and that is a sin called pride. Now God does give us free will, but that free will needs to be godly and bring glory to Him when it is in line with His will. How we do that greatly depends on how closely we walk with Him and our thoughts of reverence of Him. Acknowledge Him as *the* Authority, period. All that said, you do have some leeway in life. (More on that a little later.)

Acknowledge also means to express agreement with someone. In the context of this discussion, it means agreement with God, what Jesus did for us on the cross, and what the Holy Spirit does now. In its simplest form, the word "Amen" comes to mind, which means "so be it," or "I sincerely hope what I said is in agreement with you."

We all know how much we appreciate knowing someone agrees with us and acknowledges what we have done. God does, too, and He is glorified when we acknowledge and appreciate Him.

Acknowledge also means to make known the receipt of something. "Witnessing" is the simple term here. It means to be ready with an answer (1 Peter 3:15) and to make known what Jesus has done for us and for those who repent of their sins and accept Jesus as their Lord. Acknowledging what Jesus has done for us, and our future with Him to others, brings glory to God.

Acknowledge also means to express gratitude. Telling God "thank you" is a must for every Christian. It cannot be overstated: We must thank Him as often as we can and for as much as we can think of. Every good thing is a gift from Him (James 1:17). And when you express your gratitude, you bring glory to Him.

How close are you to God? There's one way you can tell … by how many things He does for you that you can see as well as things you pause to thank and praise Him for. The number of times you acknowledge what He does for you—or even just the beauty of what He has created around you—is directly related to how close you are to Him. The closer to Him you are, the more of His goodness you see, delight in, and acknowledge.

What we think about God is very important, and when gratitude is part of your thoughts toward God, there are some great promises He has in store for you.

"Delight yourself also in the LORD, and He shall give you the desires of your heart. Commit your way to the LORD, Trust also in Him, And He shall bring it to pass" (Psalm 37:4–5).

Acknowledging what God has done for you results in delight in God. My dad says, "There is always, always, always something to be thankful for, even if it's being thankful your heart is beating."

When you delight in God, He promises to give you the desires of your heart. A wonderful promise, isn't it?! As mentioned earlier, yours must be a heart that trusts God. God will give you the desires of your heart when your heart's desires, your innermost longings, line up with His.

The promise does say "your" ways and "your" path, not His …

So there is actually a lot of leeway there. He created you with your own mind and our own desires and wishes. You are uniquely wired with strengths, talents, and hopes and dreams. He loves to give you those desires if He will be glorified. When you are on the path He agrees with, or maybe has set before you because it's best for you, He is acknowledged with every step because that is where you are looking (all our ways), and then He is glorified.

Acknowledge also means to express an obligation to someone. Every knee shall bow, and every tongue shall confess that Jesus is Lord (Rom. 14:11; Rev. 5:13). It is more glorifying to God to do that while alive here on earth rather than after you die and do so in heaven. Philippians 2:9–11 says doing so is to the glory of God the Father.

"THAT WAS INTERESTING, BUT HOW DO I GLORIFY GOD WITH IT?"

There are over forty scriptural passages telling us to acknowledge God. When I reviewed each verse, I found a few themes. From those I came up with these ways to acknowledge Him:

- Acknowledge that He is and who He is (Heb. 11:6).
- Acknowledge who you are compared to Him (Isa. 55:8–9).
- Acknowledge His truth, not Satan's deceptions and lies (Gen. 3; John 10:10).
- Acknowledge what He has done for you (1 Cor. 6:19–20).
- Acknowledge whose life you live (Gal. 2:20).
- Acknowledge God's gifts, help, power, and strength given to you (Phil 4:6–7, 13, 19; Luke 21:36; Matt. 7:7–8; 1 Pet. 5:7; Isa. 41:10; Ps. 37:23–24).
- Acknowledge He will provide your basic needs if you seek Him and His kingdom (Matt. 6:33).
- Acknowledge Him by looking to Him and listening to Him (Pss. 32:8, 37:3).
- Acknowledge He is with you always (Matt. 28:19–20).

If it isn't already obvious, the word "acknowledge" has the word "knowledge" in it. I think that is very significant. Acknowledge comes from combining the two words "accord" and "knowledge." "According to knowledge" is the long version. We glorify God according to the knowledge we have of Him.

So, please, endeavor to know more about God. You do so by studying Him and His attributes. A good practical way to do that is to read several of the psalms. Another way is to study Jesus by reading the four Gospels. Mark is the best one to start with because it's a rapid-fire introduction to Jesus. Read it with the frame of mind of learning how Jesus acted as a person. How did He handle situations? What was His response to the various people? How did various people react to Him?

"Can I watch TV and play video games all the time?"

God gave you life for a reason. The reason is not just to pay bills and eat, nor is it to just watch TV and play video games (although some of that is okay). Acknowledge that God has plans for you and tasks for you to do for Him. Acknowledge you are His servant and you are to be fruitful and multiply ... which, by the way, means a lot more than having kids. It means to grow things, build things, improve your surroundings, improve life for other people He loves, and to enhance the world around you. It means to enhance Jesus' kingdom and the lives of those that Jesus died on the cross for.

So get off the couch and glorify God! Acknowledge Him, and do so by doing something for Him. Work well, serve well, and give well. Why not start by giving of your time? Just call your local church and simply ask, "What can I do to help someone?"

Give God a "thumbs-up"

Acknowledging God's character in your surroundings, where God's attributes can be clearly seen, is giving God a huge "thumbs-up." Appreciate and honor the complexity and beauty of His creation, such as beautiful mountains and soothing beaches, the beauty and usefulness of trees, and beautiful sunsets ... the awesomeness of the human body and His brilliant DNA structure ... the provision for our enjoyment of food ... the wonderful fulfillment and help of relationships ... the incredible gift of a godly spouse ... the reliability of His Word, the Bible.

"I like to be acknowledged, God probably does too."

I try to acknowledge God when driving to work each day. I relate to Him in the beauty of the sunrise and the distant mountains. I thank Him for the nice car I have to get to work in ... . and especially the heater on some mornings. I acknowledge His brilliantly designed wings of the bird that flew next to my car or the hooves of the deer that scampered up the hill (as I thank Him I didn't hit that deer with my car). I thank Him for the traffic laws that came from His pattern of rules to protect us, not make life difficult. I praise Him for His leading in my career and the provisions for my family that comes from it. Doing so each morning *always* lifts my spirit as I walk in the front door of my employer.

Acknowledge Jesus is LORD; in fact, bow your knee and express that. Romans 14:11 and Philippians 2:10 say everyone will bow to a knee to Jesus and say He is LORD. And it's much better to do that sooner than later. When you acknowledge Jesus is God and is Lord of your life, you bring glory to Him. A great way to acknowledge Him is to teach others about Him. Your validity of Him and His Word is most evident when you both teach it to others and mentor others using His principles. I think God's pattern for each of us is to be mentored by someone and to mentor someone. Someone "above" us to learn from, and someone "below" us to pass down our knowledge and wisdom.

God never fails to give us grace and guidance when we trust Him.
—Dr. David Jeremiah

PRACTICAL APPLICATIONS

1. Spend a few minutes each night before bed acknowledging ways God was present or helped you during that day.

2. _____

_____

3. _____

_____

7 INTEGRITY

Being honorable, honest, trustworthy, reliable, on time, and going the extra mile are all traits of *integrity* a Christian should have. Think carefully about each one of those attributes. We all can work on them and improve them in our daily life. God can use a person with a reputation of displaying those traits, as He is then glorified.

"INTEGRITY? I HAVE THAT, DON'T I?"

We think we know what integrity is, but few of us actually do.

According to Merriam Webster's Online Dictionary, integrity is (1) firm adherence to a code of especially moral or artistic values: incorruptibility; (2) an unimpaired condition: soundness; and, (3) the quality or state of being complete or undivided: completeness.[10]

To have integrity, you have to know the code of moral values to adhere to. When asked about integrity, everyone—even non-Christians—will tell you it's about following those ethics the Bible talks about. They intrinsically know there is some connection of having integrity and the Bible.

Each of those traits in the opening paragraph of this chapter comprise the part and parcel of integrity. Some of them will come easier for you than others, but never are all of them normal or effortless for any person.

You have to work at having integrity. Looking at passages in the "code manual" for having integrity (the Bible), we can learn how to work on and become known as a person with *integrity:*

- A person with integrity is one whose yes is yes and no is no as Jesus said in Matthew 5:37. In your job, give sixty minutes of work for an hour of pay. Anything less is dishonest, disingenuous, and defamatory to God.
- Be faithful to your spouse and love him or her. This, as we are told in Ephesians 5, is honorable and displays integrity. After all, you gave your word you would when you got married. Always be faithful to others, such as holding something in confidence when a friend opens up to you concerning an issue they have.
- A person with integrity does all without complaining and as if working directly for the Lord as their boss (Phil. 2:14–15; Eph. 6:5–7).
- A person with integrity honors those in authority over him or her. This includes your boss and anyone "above" you at your job. It also includes your pastors and leaders in your church who, according to 1 Timothy 5:17, are worthy of double honor, especially if they labor in the Word and doctrine. Honor your elected leaders and those in law enforcement.
- A person with integrity teaches the Word of God to their children and to those they care about (Deut. 6:6–9), controls their tongue (James 1:26), listens well (Prov. 18:13), and is slow to anger (Prov. 16:32).
- A person with integrity cares about others. They're not only strong and courageous but also humble and servant-like, many times to the point of treating others as more important than themselves. They're also merciful and forgiving when wronged. A person with integrity is like Jesus.

When your name is mentioned in conversation, do people think or say you are an honorable person? Do they think you are honest, trustworthy, and punctual? Would you be someone they would call if they really needed an honest opinion, trustworthy help, or reliable advice? If not, you need to work on those things. They need to become your nature, because they are Jesus' nature. For when your name is mentioned in conversation and the thoughts or words associated with your name contain those terms, it brings glory to God ... especially if those people know you are a *Christian*.

Proverbs 22:1 says that a good name is to be chosen over riches as it is more valuable than silver or gold. That helps when we are faced with a decision to do the honorable thing or not ... especially if the decision concerns gaining money unethically. Notice the proverb says "chosen," which means you have to consciously make the choice to have a good name. And it may cost you some riches when you do.

First Peter 2:11–12 says we are to be honorable among unbelievers. When you are with a few people after work, at a sporting event, or at a business convention, you are to maintain integrity, even when fleshly lusts want control and your friends are pressuring you to stray from your integrity. Because, as Peter goes on to say, when we hold to integrity, they will have nothing bad to say about us. In fact, he goes on to say that at some point, people will actually glorify God because of the integrity they saw in you!

WHEN GOD GIVES YOU A "THUMBS-UP"

Maintaining integrity in all you do—at home, at play, and at work—is approved by God, and it's never a waste of effort. Psalm 41:12 says, "As for me, You uphold me in my integrity, and You set me before Your face forever."

I love the word pictures this passage evokes. God will stand by you and uphold you: He'll literally hold you up when you have integrity. And you will be placed right before God so He can keep His eye on you and look out for you ... forever. I like to think we'll maybe even be close to Him in heaven, sort of like His inner circle. Think about that for a minute ... maintaining integrity is so pleasing to God, He wants you to hang out close to Him ... forever!

That psalm passage also tells me God notices me when I choose to have integrity. Maybe He even gives me a "thumbs-up" while looking directly at me. Perhaps others notice Him doing that and think to themselves, "That's a special person."

While growing up, we only had two television channels, so viewing choices were limited. I liked the original *Star Trek* where Spock had intellectual and logical integrity, while Captain James T. Kirk lacked morals but deferred to Spock's integrity from logic by the end of each show.

On the same weeknight that *Star Trek* was on, so was *Little House on the Prairie*, my sister's favorite on the other channel. So, with only one TV set and DVR not being invented yet, my sister and I had to trade off, one week my show, the next her show. Her show always taught integrity from a moral conscience; my show taught integrity from intelligence, a nice mix growing up.

Westerns were a popular genre in the 1960s and 1970s, and most of those movies or weekly shows pitted a bad guy against someone with integrity. John Wayne comes to mind as someone with integrity (or he at least *portrayed* that someone in many shows). Integrity is what makes a hero a hero.

When I was in high school in the late '70s, John Wayne was the master of ceremonies of the Fourth of July parade in Cody, Wyoming, near where I lived. I wanted so much to see him in person, this icon of manly leadership and the pinnacle of integrity. Standing on the street side among hundreds, if not thousands, of other people, waiting for the clowns in little cars to go by, waiting for the local politicians in convertibles to go by, there I was … *waiting*.

I waited until finally the horse-drawn wagon with the Duke himself, standing head and shoulders above the others riding in the wagon, came along right after the baton twirlers. He wasn't wearing a cowboy hat and still stood tall above the others. (Integrity makes you stand tall, you know.) He wore a tan suit coat with dark brown patches over the elbows. (And, yes, integrity wears a tan suit coat with brown elbow patches, so later that fall, I bought a tan suit coat with dark brown elbow patches.)

At the parade, I wanted—no, *yearned*—to be noticed by the Duke. I wanted to tell him my prepared speech; oh, yes, I had prepared words to say to John Wayne! I was going to tell him guns kick when you shoot them—they have recoil—so when he shoots a gun in front of a camera, hearing it go bang with no recoil does not bode well for a man of his level of integrity. He obviously needs to fake the effect of the recoil when the fake gun shoots fake bullets. After all, I was sixteen and knew more than John Wayne about guns, you know.

As the Duke's wagon rolled right in front of me, he turned to the other side of the street. Just then, I remembered my trip to the White House in Washington, DC, for 4-H, where I saw then-president Jimmy Carter come out of the Oval Office and walk down the hall. I only saw the back of his head. Yep, here, too, at this glorious Independence Day Parade, where heroes are honored, and I had a speck to deliver, I saw the back of John Wayne's head. He waved at someone on the other side of the street and gave them a thumbs-up. What a special person that must have been! Mr. "Duke Integrity" gave a thumbs-up to someone else with integrity.

With integrity, you are a hero to God, and He turns to *you* and waves at you in a crowd and gives you a thumbs-up!

The group of people with the highest level of integrity, those who are heroes and respected and admired by everyone, should be true Christians. That is a responsibility we need to take seriously and work as hard as we can to earn. God will be glorified when we maintain the highest level of integrity.

"WHAT EXACTLY IS INTEGRITY AND HOW DO I GET IT?"

So what exactly *is* integrity and how do we achieve it as Christians? It starts with learning biblical doctrine, then allowing that to shape our beliefs and set our values. We have to learn integrity, as it is the outpouring of our beliefs. And when we are solid in our beliefs, integrity shines through in our actions.

Our beliefs and values permeate our thoughts. Our thoughts *should* control our emotions, but both are present, battling for supremacy. And our thoughts and emotions converge in the form of words and actions. It's linear progression that must flow like this: Bible → Beliefs/Values → Thoughts → Emotions → Actions.

Let me make that a little simpler. Integrity exists when our beliefs control our actions. It's a sweet spot between the two where we all need to learn to live:

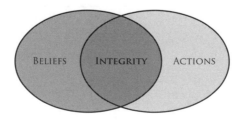

BELIEFS   INTEGRITY   ACTIONS

In his excellent book *Integrity*,"[11] Dr. Henry Cloud talks a lot about integrity and character as the ability to meet the demands of reality. He says, "That is why success and fruitfulness depend as much upon focusing on the 'who' you are as much as the 'what' of the work you do. Invest in your character, and it will give you the returns that you are looking for by only investing in the work itself. You can't do the latter without the former."

I believe the "who" you are is rooted in the "who" Jesus is. The more you become like Jesus, the more integrity you have, the more fruitful you are, and the more glorifying to God you are. This involves all of the previously stated ways to glorify God and the ones to follow in subsequent chapters. Glorifying God adequately, indeed, *gloriously*, links all of these together and, as I stated in the beginning, Jesus is the core.

Don't settle to be ordinary; endeavor to be glorious! Having integrity is how to start!

When General H. Norman Schwarzkopf was asked what was wrong with America, he said it was the lack of *integrity*. If we Christians can exhibit the utmost integrity, we can be—and *do*—wonderful things to the glory of God. We can shine noticeably as light does in the darkness, and we glorify God when we do. You can stand head and shoulders above the others in your wagon.

PRACTICAL APPLICATIONS

1. Do the right thing at work, a restaurant, or the store—even if you think it won't matter—such as giving back the change that was given to you incorrectly, taking back the pens you took home from work, and so on.

2. _____

   _____

3. _____

   _____

8 SKILLFUL

When we are good at what we do, we bring glory to God. Give your craft or job your hardest and fullest effort. Try to be the best at what you do, and give God the glory every chance you get—especially in front of others.

One of the best ways we Christians can make an impact for Christ and bring glory to God is simply by being competent, trustworthy, and "top in our field" … which I will call being *skillful*.

SKILLFUL MEANS MORE THAN YOU THINK.

Looking up the meaning of the word "skillful" or "skill" is very informative and makes this way to glorify God even more important than I first thought. Here are the various meaning of those words and how we can apply them to our life:

"Skill" (as a verb)[12]

- *To set apart, separate.* Sounds a lot like being holy, doesn't it?!
- *To discern, have knowledge or understanding, to know how.* These are traits of a mature Christian from the book of Proverbs!

- *To make a difference, or signify: To matter.* Jesus told us to be like this when He said we are to be salt and light in Matthew 5:14.

"Skill" (as a noun)[13]

- *Capacity to do something well.* This is so Jesus can say to you, "Well done, good and faithful servant."
- *Discriminating; judgment, understanding.* This sounds like being wise, companionate, "whose yes is yes, and no is no," as Jesus commanded of us!

"Skill" (as an adjective)[14]

- *Great, excellent.* So we stand out in a crowd in a way that brings glory to God!

"I DON'T THINK I HAVE A SKILL. IS THERE HOPE?"

Yes, there *is* hope. Consider these two "less than normal" guys: Joseph was an annoying, spoiled little kid with no redemptive value hated by his brothers, but he stuck with God through some very hard circumstances to becoming one of the main leaders in Egypt. He even saved his family from sure starvation and death. He learned to be skillful and added integrity, so God used him greatly and was glorified.

Daniel and his friends were kidnapped as teenagers and sent to a far-off pagan land, but they stuck to what God, their parents, and their heritage taught them. Daniel became especially skillful and intelligent, resulting in an incredible glory to God and eventual help to his people and to us!

Thank God for your abilities and for the opportunity to use them. Everyone has some good abilities. Rise above your circumstances and stick to what you know is right and what honors God. Work hard, always giving 100 percent, and you will become skillful. God approves of hard work—He invented it, He does it Himself, and He is glorified when we work hard and work skillfully. As I also know from my own life, He rewards those who work hard at being skillful at something.

My dad used to say "a job worth doing is worth doing well." It does not matter what the job is—a doctor, a truck driver, plumber, welder, software code writer, farmer, waitress, salesperson, or toilet cleaner—doing it skillfully and thankfully is glorifying to God. This even applies to tasks we do outside our job, such as hobbies or helping our neighbor or an elderly widow.

If you are a housepainter, be the best one in the valley. If you are a barista, make the best coffee drinks in town with a God-glorifying attitude. If you sew quilts, make the best looking quilts anyone has ever seen. Because people in your surroundings probably know you are a Christian (hopefully), their impression of a follower of Jesus will come from the skill you do your job or hobby.

We have been talking about being a light in a dark world. Jesus told us to in Matthew 5:16, "Let your light so shine before men, that they may see your good works and glorify your Father in heaven." What I like about that is the central point, your good works. That means being good at the work you do (skillful), as well as doing good things for others. Both of which still involve skill. And what does being skillful do? Jesus said others will notice and glorify God!

BEING SKILLFUL GETS YOU NOTICED.

People notice someone who is skillful at what they do. Sometimes very important people notice … and what a great witness to Jesus when they do!

"Do you see a man skillful in his work? He will stand before kings; he will not stand before obscure men" (Prov. 22:29 ESV).

In Psalm 33, we are told to praise God with instruments and songs, and to do so *skillfully*.

Being skillful, even in mundane tasks, can elevate those tasks to be something that glorifies God. The story from Os Guinness about his great-great-grandmother comes to mind as told in his book *The Call*.[15] Her husband was killed in Ireland's last duel. Being ostracized and ridiculed, she decided to end her life. However, her plan was stopped and she became a follower of Jesus after watching the skill of a simple plowman who took great care plowing his field because he knew, even though no one cared or noticed, God did. He elevated the mundane and probably never knew the incredible effects of plowing that field had on several generations of Christians, including readers of *The Call* and recipients of Os Guinness's great teaching. Oh, and the skillfully produced staple of Ireland, Guinness stout. (You were probably thinking of that anyway.)

How skillful a carpenter do you think Jesus was? If He made a wooden chair, did the underside of the chair look as good as the top side? I think so. I think Jesus was incredibly skillful as a carpenter before He started His ministry. In fact, I think he was so skillful that no one ever said anything negative about Him or His work, or you can rest assured we would have read about that somewhere. Some reporter would have dug up an example or found someone to come forward and say something like "Oh yeah, Jesus wasn't so great; the wall he framed in my house was crooked, and he covered it up with plaster." Nope, no one said anything like that at all because Jesus was incredibly skillful. That skill and attention to all aspects of a job well done is what partly defines *skill*.

In Exodus 35 through 39, you will read of a lot of people chosen because they were skillful to make the Tabernacle, the ark, and related items. Some even got their names in the Bible. Wouldn't that have been cool ... being so skillful you are mentioned in God's Word? Verse 35 says God filled them with skill to do all manner of work. We can probably infer that if God calls someone to do work for Him, He will give them the skill and tools to do it, including sufficient strength when they don't think they have it.

I also think skill comes from God so we don't become prideful. Therefore, our skill can bring glory to God instead of to us. It's because of Him we are skillful.

Humility is hard when we become good at something, but when our perspective is proper, humility is exactly how we glorify Him. Paul says in 1 Thessalonians 4:11 to "aspire to lead a quiet life, to mind your own business, and to work with your own hands," so obedience to that will glorify God.

WORK IS A GIFT FROM GOD.

God created work for us all to do and is the main place where we Christians can shine as lights in a dark world (Phil. 2:15), especially if we are good at what we do, commanding respect and admiration.

God gave us the gift of work for many reasons. Here are several:

- Because God Himself works: He worked for six days creating things and rested on the seventh. We are created in His image, and we are to imitate Him like a mirror image. "Therefore be imitators of God as dear children" (Eph. 5:1).

- We are to be fruitful and multiply. We are also to be creative and improve our surroundings, all for the betterment of ourselves and other people God loves. "Then God blessed them, and God said to them, "Be fruitful and multiply; fill the earth and subdue it" (Gen. 1:28).
- We are to form relationships with other people—partly to spread the gospel, partly to help others, partly to be helped *by* others. It gives a venue to be salt and light. "Let your light so shine before men, that they may see your good works and glorify your Father in heaven" (Matt. 5:13–16).
- It teaches us to rely on God and need His help (Ps. 37:5).
- It builds our relationship with Him (Ps. 55:22), and it teaches us to trust Him (Ps. 56:3–4).
- Dozens of scriptural passages become real and impactful to us through our jobs (including Rom. 8:28–29 and others).
- It gives us a venue to use the gifts, abilities, and talents God gives us. "So he who had received five talents came and brought five other talents, saying, 'Lord, you delivered to me five talents; look, I have gained five more talents besides them.' His lord said to him, 'Well done, good and faithful servant; you were faithful over a few things, I will make you ruler over many things. Enter into the joy of your lord'" (Matt. 25:14–30).
- It gives us opportunities to glorify God. "Therefore, whether you eat or drink, or whatever you do, do all to the glory of God" (1 Cor. 10:31).
- It provides the monetary income necessary in our society to meet our needs and the needs of our families, and some of our wants.
- It provides the monetary income from which to tithe and support ministries. "On the first day of the week let each one of you lay something aside, storing up as he may prosper" (1 Cor.16:2).
- It provides money and items to give to those in need. "Let him who stole steal no longer, but rather let him labor, working with his hands what is good, that he may have something to give him who has need" (Eph. 4:28).
- It makes for a good night's sleep. "The sleep of a laboring man is sweet, Whether he eats little or much" (Eccles. 5:12).

When you look over those reasons and the corresponding biblical passages, did you notice the one that did not have a Bible reference? Isn't it interesting that of the dozen reasons we work stated in Scripture, the one we concentrate on the most has no Bible reference? To me, that is a clear statement as to what is more important to *us* is not so important to God! So it could be we need to reevaluate why we work and do so more biblically aligned with God's view and trusting Him.

Jesus talked about this inaccurate priority in Matthew 6 where He said in verses 25 and 33: "I say to you stop worrying about your life … what you will eat … or wear … But seek first the kingdom of God and His righteousness, and all these things shall be added to you." The term "kingdom" in this context is basically saying we are to pursue things that matter to God. Things that glorify Him.

We can become so wrapped up in how much money we make in our job that we completely ignore what purposes God has for us in our job and how we can glorify Him at work. Just realize that for most of us, our views of work and our reasons to work generally do not align with Scripture.

Glorifying God is not something you do only in church on Sunday and during your small group meetings on Thursday night. Glorifying God is done during *all* waking hours, and the majority of those hours (for most of us) are spent working. You glorify God at work, and the number one way to do so is to be skillful in our job.

HOW TO BECOME SKILLFUL

- Humble yourself. Be willing to learn. Ask questions.
- Learn from mistakes, which begins with admitting you made a mistake.
- Learn from someone who is skillful at something.
- Take notes. Refer to your notes.
- Commit to something. Pick one or more things and get really, really good at it.
- Failure is a way of learning, so reduce your failures and improve your success rate. If you are 65 percent successful, work up to 95 percent or so.
- Google it … watch YouTube videos … read … take classes … learn all you can. Then *do* it.

- Hard work, practice, and patience always pay off.
- Practice, practice, practice.
- Exude patience, patience, patience.
- Stretch and work until you are tired. That's how you learn and get better.
- Learn what you are good at and do that. Know what you are *not* good at and just stay away from it, unless you really want to master it.

WHAT WILL THE RESULTS BE FOR YOUR EFFORTS?

When you are skillful at what you do, here are the results:

- Your morale is better.
- You have more motivation.
- You have more confidence.
- You are more in control.
- You are happier.
- You feel support by those around you.
- You are less apt to doubt, worry, and be fearful.

Which of these results bring glory to God? *All of them.*

TOOLS OF THE SKILLFUL

Being skillful involves your use of tools or abilities. Become skillful at the tools of the trade, then you can be skillful at your job. Learn the history of your tools how to properly use them, and, if possible, effective ways to use them "outside of the box" to accomplish tasks others struggle with.

The first tool that comes to mind is our body and our spirit. First Corinthians 6:20 says we are to "glorify God in your body and in your spirit, which are God's." To me, that means take care of *your body* so it will serve God well and glorify Him. Eat well, exercise, get regular check-ups.

Your spirit means your attitude. Have a "gung-ho" demeanor about you for glorifying God in all you do, sort of like a beaming light. Others will notice both of these traits and may also glorify God as Matthew 5:16 says:, "Let your light so shine before others that they may see your good works and glorify your Father in heaven."

The use of Scripture correctly is one tool every Christian must endeavor to use and hone. Become skillful in Scripture. God can really use a person who knows Him and His Word. Become skillful in the concepts and specifics of Scripture, the Word of Truth. The apostle Paul said in 2 Timothy 3:16–17, "All Scripture is given by inspiration of God, and is profitable for doctrine, for reproof, for correction, for instruction in righteousness, that the man of God may be complete, thoroughly equipped for every good work." Notice he said, "thoroughly equipped for every good work." What is your work? Scripture can be used in your work.

The Bible is a huge book, and it's daunting, I know. So I would suggest you pick a book in the Bible and master it. Become skillful with that book. I remember Dr. John MacArthur, pastor at Grace Community Church in California, saying he wanted to really master the book of 1 John. So he read through it once a day for thirty days. It's a short book, so even you could do that. He continued to say that after thirty days, he enjoyed reading it so much, seemingly learning something new every day, that he kept reading it daily for another thirty or so days! He became very skillful at teaching, answering questions, and quoting from 1 John. The concepts in 1 John help everyone, regardless of whether you're a plumber, an architect, or a secretary.

The Christian shoemaker does his duty not by putting little crosses on the shoes, but by making good shoes.
—Martin Luther

PRACTICAL APPLICATIONS

1. Practice, read, view how-to videos, and so on to become the best at something you can do at your job (where you spend the most waking time of your week).

2. _____

   _____

3. _____

   _____

9 INFLUENCE

We are commanded to be a light into a dark world (Matt. 5:14–16). We are to make a godly impact for Christ in all we say and do, to be an *influence* where God has placed us and with those people He brings into our lives. This word is the *essence* of being a Christian and is one of the main ways we can glorify God.

INFLUENCE LIKE SALT AND LIGHT

The meaning of the word "influence" is to have an effect on the character, development, or behavior of someone. That means at home with your family, while visiting your relatives, and even at your job with your coworkers. Everyone is an influence on someone else, so please make your influence such that God is glorified … or at least pleased. You may get a personal evaluation from Jesus, and one of the topics of discussion will be how you influenced the people He brought into your path for Him.

I believe God brings people into our lives we are to influence for Him. Jesus used the term "salt and light" because salt seasons food to make it better. It also kills germs and weeds. Light helps us to see more clearly when it's dark as it helps keep us from stumbling and helps us find our way.

In every part of life, we are to be God's light in a dark world. When His light shines through us, we will influence others. Stand for—and be known for—what is light, not what is dark. Another way of saying that is, be known for what you are *for* more than for what you are *against*.

DO YOU SPARKLE?

When I picked out the wedding ring for my wife, I had an idea of the style I wanted and sort of knew what it should look like. While at the jewelers, I saw several that met what I was looking for, all of which were twice the price I could afford. But I was marrying "up," so that was acceptable. Just as sweat beads formed on my forehead (as if I just ate spicy habanero sauce), and oxygen became scarce in the sales room, a slick, Porsche-driving salesman came over and asked if I wanted to see one, so I pointed and said, "Yes, please, one of those three there," as I pointed to a row of rings.

The salesman was very good, and before he pulled a ring out of the case, he laid a black velour cloth on the counter. He took one of the rings out of the case—the most expensive, of course—hence the Porsche in the parking lot. Side note: If you are in sales, drive a rusty old car to work, which gives the impression of low margins. But this guy was better than most: he parked his Porsche right up front, with a vanity license plate reading "MARKUP."

He swung over a bright light as he set the ring on the black cloth. The gestures of his hands as they left the ring to dazzle me communicated the ring held the famed Pink Panther diamond. Under the light, and against the black velour backdrop, the ring seemed to come alive and sparkle like it was battery operated. I was struck by the sparkle, like a hippie in Spencer's black light room, and blurted out without even thinking, "That's the one. I'll take it!"

If you know how a diamond is cut and mounted, then you'll know the available light comes from underneath the stone and shines through it toward you with a magnificent sparkle. I was *influenced*, but not by the bright light or the ring itself, and not by the ring against the black cloth. I was influenced by the sparkle in the ring from the light shining through it, accented by the contrast of the black cloth.

Our Christian life is like that. A diamond is a lump of coal that has been put under heat and pressure. Then a jeweler cuts the stone precisely and uniformly to get it to the shape needed to sparkle in a diamond ring. It doesn't sparkle unless there is a brilliant light shining through it. We are to let God's light shine through us, and among the dark backdrop of our world, that sparkle is very influential! Are you using your influence to inspire others as a diamond?

Being a godly influence on others, like the sparkle from a diamond, brings glory to God and enhances God's kingdom, which we are commanded by Jesus to do in Matthew 6:33 when we use what God has entrusted to us: His truth, His knowledge, His wisdom, and His attributes through the gifts He gives us to the people He puts in our path.

"CAN YOU EXPLAIN HOW?"

Being an influence on others from a biblical point of view of God shining through us involves sharing the gospel of Jesus to others, helping people grow and mature as Christians. That's called "making disciples," which is the last command Jesus gave us in Matthew 28:18–20.

Being an influence on others means being someone who is pleasant to be around, someone who seems to love others. The best way I know is to treat others with grace, compassion, and care, forgiving them when they wrong you. God will judge others, usually, so you don't have to, but you can care about them. Colossians 3:12 says to "put on tender mercies, kindness, humility, meekness, longsuffering; bearing with one another, and forgiving one another." Ephesians 4:32 similarly tells us to "be kind to one another, tenderhearted, forgiving one another, even as God in Christ forgave you."

Being an influence is to be generous. Giving is influential. It includes your time, your ear (listening, such as Ephesians 6:2 says), and your services (such as for widows and orphans and others in need), as James 1:27 says. Giving to charity and organizations and missions is fantastic and influential. Helping those in need, especially those in your family and household, as 1 Timothy 5:8 says, is your priority. Doing so lovingly, happily, and as if doing so for Jesus, as Matthew 25:45 says, is tantamount.

"AND TELL ME WHO TO ...?"

First and foremost, we are to care for and be a godly influence to those members of our family. First Timothy 5:8 says, "But if anyone does not provide for his own, and especially for those of his household, he has denied the faith and is worse than an unbeliever." Serious stuff, isn't it?! The word "provide" in that passage means more than money; it includes everything God wants for your family should come from you—or through you—from Him.

The pattern seen in Scripture is clear: we are to mentor or influence someone, and we are to be influenced by someone. Sometimes that's hard, but when it's hard to do or even hard to for certain people, do so as if for the Lord. How and who are you influencing? Who is influencing you?

I think we all have an effect on people we are in contact with. It's either positive or negative. I would argue if your influence is not positive, then it's negative. You either give to others or take away from others. You fill their bucket or drain their bucket. I got that bucket metaphor from a book called *How Full Is Your Bucket?* by Tom Rath and Donald O. Clifton, where the "bucket" is a metaphor for a person's sense of well-being or joy, and you have a psychological dipper you use to take away from someone's bucket or add to it by your words and/or actions: The choice is yours. You glorify God when you add to another's bucket.

GOD DESERVES AN ROI.

God has invested a lot into you, but are you giving God a return on His investment? You are like a servant who has gone through a lot of training and should now be useful to the Master. Are you useful to Him? When we get to heaven, we *want* to hear "Well done, good and faithful servant." Will you? (See Matthew 25 for these words from the servant's Master.)

There are five parts to that commendation when we consider your influence on other people:

1. *Well.* Doing well as God requires and to His standards, treating others well.
2. *Done.* Are you getting done what He has called you to do? Are you influencing the people God brings into your life? Did you accomplish what He brought them to you for?
3. *Good.* Do you do good for others? Are you good at what you do? Are you a good influence on others? Did you have the aroma of Christ? Do people see hope in you?
4. *Faithful.* Are you faithful to God and His Word when serving others? Are you faithful at recognizing whom to be an influence to?

5. *Servant.* Servants anticipate their master's wishes and perform their duties without asking. Do you? A good servant serves their master and others, not themselves. Do you serve others even when you are uncomfortable? Do you obey without complaining? And does this include Jesus?

When we are at work and do a great job in every way, the boss looks good, right?! And, he or she probably takes the credit. Similarly, God "looks good" (is glorified) when we do the same during our time here on earth.

YOUR SPHERE OF INFLUENCE

Being useful to God will make a great impact on those around you. That's called your *sphere of influence.* Who is in your "sphere of influence"? Can you name them? Using the pattern of Jesus, write down their names:

Name the 3 people who are closest to you.
1.
2.
3.
Who are the next 9 closest people in your sphere of influence (to make a total of 12)?
4.
5.
6.
7.
8.
9.
10.
11.
12.

God has placed each one of those in your life so you can be a godly influence to them … maybe even to lead them to Jesus and help them grow in Christ. How are you doing with your responsibility?

Here is something to consider, if you can: How many people will come to your funeral and want to say good things about you and the influence you were on their life? Better yet, how many people will come up to you in heaven and give you a hug and say, "I am here because of Jesus, but *you* led me to Him … thank you!"

How can we be influential in a way that glorifies God? Here are several practical application ways to be an influencer:

- Develop relationships. Be a compassionate, good friend, and show love to others.
- Have joy. Joy is different than being happy. You can be unhappy but still have joy. Joy should be emanating from you as a sweet aroma. People should sense your joy.
- Have a positive attitude. If you look for the negative, you will find it and be it. But if you look for positives, you will be positive, and others will want to be around you. Be a positive tone-setter.
- Be gracious. God has been gracious to you through Jesus; you can be gracious to others too.
- Spend Sabbath★ time with those in your sphere of influence.
- Be confident. As God encouraged Joshua, be strong and courageous.
- Be knowledgeable. As Solomon tells us in Proverbs, attain and love biblical knowledge. Read passages in the Bible as often as you can.
- Practice practical application of those Bible passages in your life.
- Be ready. Have an answer when anyone asks you about the hope that you have.

THE INFLUENCE OF TAKING YOUR WATCH OFF

Sabbath time★ is something God Himself instituted, and I think it should be done more than one day a week. Here is what I mean: Sabbath time is a period of time to just relax, stop, rest, sit, listen, and give time and attention to God *and* others. It's a time to communicate positively. To give God *and* someone your time. To show God *and* others you recognize them, and they have more value to you than you. Rest with them, hold them close, and let them know how precious they are to you.

A few years ago, God taught me a lesson on the concepts of Sabbath and influencing people. In the construction industry, price estimates from subcontractors and suppliers are usually due to the general contractor on a specific day and time, such as 10:00 a.m. on Thursday, March 5. You get your bid in to them before that time or it won't be considered. As a structural steel estimator, I get into a "zone" while bidding and cannot be bothered as I finalize a bid, especially if the due date and time is rapidly approaching.

While once in that frantic time finishing up a bid, one of our welders came to my office and said, "Hey, Kevin, can I talk to you for a few minutes?" I recognized his voice but didn't even look up from my drawings and computer screen as I shot back a reply of, "No, Scott, can't you see I have a bid due?!" Shortly afterward, our shop foreman paged me and said that the welder had just quit and driven away. I never knew why, or what was bothering him, I just knew I had a chance to be an influence on him, and I blew it. The next morning the shop was abuzz with the news his dead body was found in his rolled truck at an "S curve" near town.

As I heard this additional heart-wrenching news about Scott, my head and heart sank as tears welled up in my eyes and I realized, God cared more about that young man than the bid I was working on ... which by the way, I was not awarded. I let that young man down, members of his family down, our company down, and I *really* let God down. From that day on, if someone comes into my office and asks to talk, I take a "Sabbath" break; I close the door, pull up my chair next to him/her, *take my watch off of my wrist*, and set it behind me face down, and give that person my full untimed attention.

Influence starts by showing love (see chapter 3). It works best when communication is two way, or you maybe even listen to them more than you talk to them. Don't think about what you are going to say next while the person in front of you is still talking ... they will know it and not feel influenced.

THE INFLUENCE OF PICKING SOMEONE UP

I came back into the office from being out in the shop one day with my arm, chest, and side of my face dirty. Dark-gray dirty, and one of our wonderful office ladies asked, "Did you fall down out there?" to which I replied, "No, I picked someone up."

I had gone out to the shop to check on the status of a job for a customer, and I noticed one of our welders seemed down. I stopped and mentioned he didn't seem his usual self that day ... to which he replied his girlfriend had left him the night before. The ensuing Holy Spirit-induced conversation was wonderful, and I ended up telling him I would be praying for him, and her, and gave him a hug ... hence the dirtiness on my clothes and face.

Being an influence that glorifies God means you may have to intentionally engage a person and be willing to get dirty with them.

People for you to influence for God are all around you, even at home, where you shouldn't let your influence down. Influence your spouse—*especially* your spouse. Or influence your roommate. And then there are your kids. This probably needs its own book: You parents are training the next generation, and your children are your most important influence. What will that influence be?

Here is a little side note: I have noticed that lazy people use humor to build themselves up and devalue others. Really intelligent people who care and love others deeply use humor to influence others by elevating them. I only bring that up to point out humor is a great tool, but only when it builds others up and cuts no one down. Don't use humor at the expense of someone else unless they are standing right there, and you cleared it with them at some time prior.

Witnessing to others, leading them to their need of repentance of sins, and accepting Jesus Christ as their Lord and Savior is the ultimate "influence." It's also possibly the best way to glorify Him. From there, mentor those people to ensure their growth in the Lord and that their lives are fruitful for Him.

Blessed is the influence of one true, loving human soul on another.
—George Eliot

PRACTICAL APPLICATIONS

1. Whom will you make an effort to listen to today?

2. _____

   _____

3. _____

   _____

10 IMAGE

Genesis 1:26–27 says, "Then God said, 'Let Us make man in Our image, according to Our likeness; So God created man in His own image; in the image of God He created him; male and female He created them.'" We are the *image of God*. He wants us to get it; after all, He said it three times there!

THE MEANING OF "IMAGE"

It is important, therefore, to understand the meaning of the word "image." According to Merriam Webster's Online Dictionary, image, in the context of our study, means: (a): exact likeness: Semblance (or appearance).[16] I also like to get the meaning of words from the Bible, specifically the Hebrew (Old Testament) or Greek (New Testament). So I first see where else in the Bible the word is used and see what I can learn from those contexts, then I look up the word in *Strong's Concordance* to ensure it is the same word … and also to see its original meaning. Here is a good example:

Genesis 5:1–2 says, "This is the book of the genealogy of Adam. In the day that God created man, He made him in the likeness of God. He created them male and female, and blessed them and called them Mankind in the day they were created. And Adam lived one hundred and thirty years, and begot a son in his own likeness, after his image, and named him Seth."

Tseh'-lem: Meaning to shade; a phantom, that is, (figuratively) illusion, resemblance; hence a representative figure.[17] I looked up this original Hebrew meaning of the word "image" in *Strong's Concordance* as well as the other places in Scripture it is used. What came to my mind was our reflection in a mirror. Sort of like when God looks at us, he sees a reflection of Himself. That may not be *the* meaning of the word, but it is a part of the meaning, I think. When we look at ourself in the mirror, what do we do? We fix things to make us look better. God does that with us too … He fixes us and makes us better.

So just like I'd gather ingredients to make a cake, I gathered the four meanings of the word "image" and mixed them together: Likeness, resemblance, representative figure, and reflection. When cooked, what came out of the oven was one word: *imitation.*

When you sit back and let that sink in, it should scare you because of all the ramifications. It's all about accountability. We are to endeavor to be like Him. God is glorified when we are an imitation of Him, at least as accurately as we can be.

Imitation is the sincerest form of flattery, and we glorify Him when our character, attributes, actions, attitude, demeanor, deeds, and especially our relationships are an imitation of His. Now, we can't do a very good job unless there is a book of directions for us to read and follow. There is: it's the Word of God, the Bible.

In addition to that, and because many of us have a hard time reading and doing what we have read, we need a pattern to follow. If you are sewing a dress, a pattern is followed. If you need to fix your car, you watch a YouTube video of someone who successfully fixed the same problem. We need a standard to look to, like a model or hero, or, better yet, a person who already imitates God so well we can follow their lead. God gave us not only an imitation of Himself we can see but also gave us *Himself:* Jesus.

Our role model of being the image of God is His Son, Jesus, who lived here on Earth as one of us. In fact, He was not only our role model but also the very catalyst and reason for our relationship with God. Jesus is the reason we can be part of God's family and relate to Him, receiving benefits of that family relationship. The Latin phrase *Imago Dei Coram Deo* captures the gist of the issue: It means Jesus is the center of our acknowledging that God created us in His image and wants us to be like Him so He can have a relationship with us.

Jesus is paramount.

"In the beginning was the Word, and the Word was with God, and the Word was God ... And the Word became flesh and dwelt among us, and we beheld His glory, the glory as of the only begotten of the Father, full of grace and truth" (John 1:1, 14).

Recall in Genesis 1:26: "God said, 'Let Us make man in Our image, according to Our likeness.'" The "our" includes Jesus. This is the first reference the *one* God existing in three persons, the Father, the Son—Jesus—and the Holy Spirit. Jesus is God and is the tangible person we can emulate.

There are thirty Bible verses that say we are to endeavor to become like Jesus Christ, and one of them, Romans 8:29, says we are to conform to the "image" of Jesus Christ. When you look in the mirror, you see a reflection of yourself. We are to be like a mirror where God sees a reflection of Himself and, to be more specific, He sees someone just like Jesus, who is God in the flesh. Are you a mirror with that reflection? Would others say you are the image of Jesus? Not that you look like one of the Bee Gees, but your personal traits and how you interact with others, are like Jesus. When reading the Romans 8:29 passage about being like Jesus, did you notice the verse just prior to it? God causes all things, good and bad, to work together for good to those who love God and are trying to follow His purpose. That purpose is to be like Jesus ... to *conform* (be molded into) be the image of God.

That word picture of being like a mirror image of Jesus reminds me of this relevant passage in 2 Corinthians 3:18, which says when we are genuinely like Jesus and being helped to do so by the Holy Spirit, we shine with glory, reflecting back to God! "But we all, with unveiled face, beholding as in a mirror the glory of the Lord, are being transformed into the same image from glory to glory, just as by the Spirit of the Lord."

Since Jesus is God who came and dwelled among us (John 1:14), we can bring glory to Him by studying what He is like, learning about his character and His attributes. Then we can actively practice those attributes ourselves in how we act and treat others. I would suggest you take out a piece of paper and list the character traits and attributes of God (psalms have many, such as those found in Ps. 86:15) and of Jesus (reading about Jesus in the four Gospels helps) and try to portray those traits or attributes throughout the day. Doing that until they are habits and become *your* character traits and attributes will bring glory to God.

In John 17, Jesus prayed for himself, His disciples, and for us. The theme in Jesus' prayer is twofold: unity among God, Jesus, and us believers, and the glory of God, Jesus, and us. Unity and being like Jesus are closely related and are tied together with glory.

AN ALIVE IMAGE

God gives us life. Jesus died on the cross in our place so we can have life. The Enemy gives death, and that came to us during the fall in the Garden of Eden, though God warned it would come if Adam and Eve disobeyed His one requirement. Jesus talked about that in John 10:10, and He ends that sour verse with the something so sweet, we miss it. Jesus came to give us life … and to have it more abundantly.

It is the glory of God to give life. And, therefore, we bring glory to God when we are full of life. I am reminded of a quote of St. Irenaeus of Lyons (a student of Polycarp who was taught by the apostle John): "Man fully alive is the glory of God."

Being fully alive is to live life more abundantly as Jesus said. Yes, a life that is full, joyous, fun, stimulating, embracing, engaging, enterprising, loving, emotional, and charismatic—as in charming, fascinating, fun, and exciting. Yes, I said "fun" twice! As I think about Jesus' quote of John 10:10, I realized Jesus lived life more fully and abundantly than most people in that day. Don't you think so too? Jesus' full and abundant (and fun) life angered the religious people of His day, the Pharisees, and many of our religious leaders today seem to think having a full and abundant life is not spiritual. Jesus and I disagree. An abundant life is centered in Jesus, not religion.

When Jesus said in John 10:10 that through Him, we can have life and have it abundantly, He didn't only mean eternal life in heaven; He meant now, too. The word "eternal" in the phrase "eternal life" is both an adjective *and* a noun. It's a way of life now, a quality of life now, as well as in the future … living forever.

Jesus is fully human and fully God. I think we image God by being like the human Jesus. We can identify with Jesus because he lived like us, experiencing many of the same issues we have. "Identify with" is very similar to "image." So let's be human, fully alive, and enjoy life. When we do—when we live fully—we begin to see the gospel of God more fully. And as with the good news, verses like Romans 8:28–29 become real and dwell in us richly. We see others and situations in life as God does. People will rise up and call you blessed. We begin to bring glory to Him as He intended.

In our adult Sunday school class, I asked people to shout out single words describing God and His attributes or character qualities, and I wrote them down on a white board. Here's what we came up with:

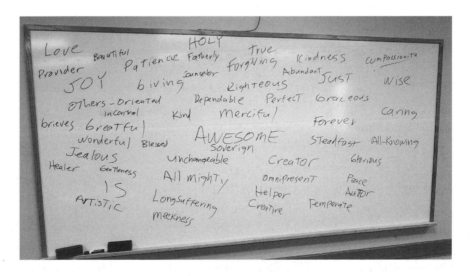

Now, since we are to be an image of God, which words above would describe us as well?

Pick some of them and ask yourself if you exemplify them. If you do, then you image God well, which brings glory to Him!

Are you compassionate? Kind? Patient? Giving? Loving? Forgiving? Gracious?

Do people around you see those attributes? Would they say they see an image of God in you? Remember the scary accountability mentioned earlier? It's totally possible to be an image of God: We have His Word; we also have Jesus to emulate. We can do this. We *should* do it. It pleases God when we are like Jesus, and it glorifies Him.

Are you the image of God on Sunday morning only, but not on Monday or Tuesday or ...? Is your image of God dependent on whom you are with? Don't be a false, phony image. Don't be an actor; don't be a hypocrite. Be the real deal, the real image of the real God, using the real role model of Jesus. I often try to think how to do that, how to be like Jesus. I mean really, practically, in my life where God has me. Sounds like a wonderful goal until you really try to put blue jeans on that concept and go to work in your job or have dinner with the in-laws. So this may help you, which it certainly has for me, do the ministry of Jesus.

DOING JESUS' MINISTRY

What does it mean to do the ministry of Jesus? Well, you can't be *like* Jesus if you aren't doing the things Jesus did. No, you probably can't heal the paraplegic or give sight to someone blind from birth, but you can do most other things Jesus did. Let's look at what Jesus Himself said His ministry and purpose actually was.

While in the temple in Nazareth, Jesus was handed part of the Bible and He read from it. He then sat down and said what He just read was his purpose and why He was there.

And He was handed the book of the prophet Isaiah. And when He had opened the book, He found the place where it was written: "The spirit of the Lord is upon me, because He has anointed me to preach the gospel to the poor; he has sent me to heal the brokenhearted, to proclaim liberty to the captives and recovery of sight to the blind, to set at liberty those who are oppressed; to proclaim the acceptable year of the Lord." Then He closed the book, and gave it back to the attendant and sat down. And the eyes of all who were in the synagogue were fixed on Him. And He began to say to them, "Today this Scripture is fulfilled in your hearing." (Luke 4:17–21)

You glorify God by being an image of Jesus through practicing the attributes in that passage:

- The Spirit of the LORD is upon you. You have the Holy Spirit to help you and prompt you to be like Jesus. Spirit also means to incorporate a Jesus-like fervor, to adopt "the essence of" the LORD, or the same frame of mind as Jesus.
- You are to preach the gospel (good news) to those who are both monetarily and spiritually poor.
- Find ways to heal (help recover) the brokenhearted, someone who lost a loved one, lost a job, and so on. You can help ease that which has broken their heart, even if it's just to empathize with them.
- Help free those held captive by sin, fear, anxiety, depression, alcoholism, or other addiction, and so on. The truth (of the Bible) can set them free.
- Help those unable to see Jesus (blinded by the world) see Him in you, and help them understand the Bible.
- Help set free those who are oppressed. Maybe they are without a job, are in a detrimental relationship, in a legalistic church, a church that requires doing works to be saved, oppressed by huge debt, or even extreme self-centeredness. Find ways to bring justice to those who have been hurt.
- Proclaim the kingdom of Jesus to give people a sampling of what God has in store for us and their future in heaven. The year of the Lord will have freedom from sin, hope, joy, peace, and love! Those things people all long for.

I am sure you can add to each one of these as they relate to your life and those you interact with. The point is, you can be like Jesus, practically speaking, and make an impact for Him to those around you. You can be a mirror image of Jesus.

BE A PINK SPOON.

Most of you have been to Baskin-Robbins ice cream shop and been given that little pink spoon with a sample of one or more of the flavors. Whoever received a sample always wanted more. I often think of that as an analogy of giving people a sampling of the kingdom of God. Show them a little now what it will be like. Show them the fruits of the spirit: love, joy, peace, patience, goodness, kindness, gentleness, and self-control. Notice which is first … and the others work because of it: love.

God's grace and mercy, through the work of Jesus, allows us to live eternally—with Him. We often think of that to mean in heaven, but it also includes our life here and now as well. When we live the abundant full life as God intends and as Jesus made possible and told us and modeled for us, we bring glory to God. We image Jesus. "For you were bought at a price; therefore glorify God in your body and in your spirit, which are God's" (1 Cor. 6:20).

"But when one turns to the Lord, the veil is removed. Now the Lord is the Spirit, and where the Spirit of the Lord is, there is freedom. And we all, with unveiled face, beholding the glory of the Lord, are being transformed into the same image from one degree of glory to another. For this comes from the Lord who is the Spirit" (2 Cor. 3:16–18).

Nothing in God's creation is devoid of splendor and ordinary … nor should you be, for you are the magnificent, glorious image of God! Live like it!

You particularly image Christ by looking out for the well-being of those God has placed within your care.
—David Powlison

PRACTICAL APPLICATIONS

1. Lighten up. Trust the God who loves you and who made you in His image! Live life fully in God's grace, mercy, and knowledge with the full assurance of spending eternity with Him!

2. _____

   _____

3. _____

   _____

11 SUFFERING

While I was studying the Bible for ways to glorify God, *suffering as a Christian* kept showing up. I would dismiss those passages and focus on other ways because it's difficult to grasp how suffering can glorify God. But I kept coming back to them and, subsequently, the reasons became clear. Suffering can be something *God* allows or causes to get our attention and to accomplish His purposes in our life or in the lives of others. Ultimately, God wins and is glorified.

Bad things happen to good people. That's just a product of the fall of Adam and Eve: The world we live in is not what it's supposed to be; it's the result of disobedience. There will come a time when bad things won't happen anymore, and God will wipe away all tears—it'll be when Satan is put in his place, and Jesus reigns as King.

In the meantime, however, God honors His promise of Romans 8:28, causing all things to work together for good. I have seen God work out some very bad things that have happened to me for my own betterment, and He is glorified.

Through those trials, I found the root of my faith went very deep, and I became better and stronger because of the trial. I am, as a result of that experience, also able to help others through similar trials. Here is something few people consider: God takes a rough occurrence, probably brought on by Satan somehow, and turns it into good for you and for Him ... so He wins. He *wins*! And He gets the glory!

First Peter 4:16 describes persistence ... and admittedly is somewhat obnoxious: "Yet if anyone suffers as a Christian, let him not be ashamed, but let him glorify God in this matter." Maybe I was ashamed of the topic of suffering, maybe I just didn't want to delve into it, but I'm glad I did. Although this isn't an exhaustive study on the topic, you will be gladdened at what you learn here too.

SUFFERING EXAMPLES FROM HISTORY

Some of the most influential Christians in history suffered greatly, and through their experiences, and how the Holy Spirit spoke through them (as promised in Mark 13:11), here are two examples that come to mind:

* Perpetua was a woman in the early church whose influential words and deeds through suffering for Christ inspired and furthered the gospel, even to this day. Two famous sayings have solidified and inspired Christians: When in prison, she was asked by her loving father to recant her Christianity in exchange for her freedom. In response, she said, "Father, do you see this vase here? Could it be called by any other name than what it is?" "No," he replied. "Well," she said, "neither can I be called anything other than what I am, a Christian."

    As to her impending execution for being a Christian in North Africa (and a testament to her trust in God), she said: "It will all happen in the prisoner's dock as God wills, for you may be sure that we are not left to ourselves but are all in his power."
* George Wishart, a pastor in Scotland in the 1500s, was burned at the stake by unbiblical church leaders. His words through his suffering during his trial are the most astonishing and influential words ever spoken to cause men afterward to focus on the Word of God. "The cause why I suffer this day is not for any crime (though I acknowledge myself a miserable sinner) but only for the defense of the truth as it is in Jesus Christ; and I praise God who hath called me, by His

mercy, to seal the truth with my life; which, as I received it from Him, so I willingly and joyfully offer it up to His glory."

You cannot read of what these people said and did and not be inspired, then fully realize suffering *for* God is a way to *glorify* God. Suffering does not mean getting a flat tire on the way to church. It means speaking and maintaining God's truth when others oppose it and are mean to you. Suffering is going through hardships because we live in this fallen world, or it's a result of the consequences of the sins of others ... and we glorify God anyway.

Bringing glory to God in our suffering comes from our actions and especially our words. Reading the godly words of those people above is amazing. Showing our trust in God, our love of Jesus, and our overall biblical view is what people notice. Some may be concerned about not doing well if our suffering gets to an extreme state. To answer that, take notice of what Jesus said in Mark 13:11: "But when they arrest you and deliver you up, do not worry beforehand, or premeditate what you will speak. But whatever is given you in that hour, speak that; for it is not you who speak, but the Holy Spirit."

John 15 is a great chapter on how to glorify God, and in verses 18 through 25, Jesus talks about suffering. Read those wonderful words yourself and learn about glorifying God by adhering to Jesus.

"DOES GOD BRING US SUFFERING"?

Does God purposefully allow suffering? Charles Stanley said, "The comfortable, but theologically incorrect, answer is no. You will find many people preaching and teaching that God never sends an ill wind into a person's life, but that position can't be justified by Scripture. The Bible teaches that God does send adversity – but within certain parameters and always for a reason that relates to our growth, perfection, and eternal good."[18]

Did God send the suffering to Job? He certainly allowed it and possibly did to prove to Satan that Job would not turn his back on God or say things against God. Job 42:11 says God brought adversity to him. Actually, chapter 42 is a wonderful passage to read on how to handle suffering and how to console those who are. Notice that Job said what is right, remained a servant of God, and repented of some sinful behavior. Even though Job went through some horrible things and lost some dear people, when the suffering ended, God richly blessed him, as you can read in Job 42:10–17.

We have to always remember that suffering is a result of our sinful world. Things could be a lot worse, but God is restraining a lot of it. There may be a long line of people in heaven wanting to punch Adam for bringing this sin and suffering on us (although Jesus will probably be there to say he already took care of what Adam should get). We also have to remember God can, in His awesomeness and power and for His glory, turn all suffering to work for good (Rom.8:28–29), and this is so important as well:

- John 10:10 says Satan comes to steal, kill, and destroy. Jesus comes to give life.
- James 1:16–17 says to not be deceived by Satan (the Great Deceiver). Every good thing is a gift that comes down from the Father, who is totally reliable.

With that said, God did allow the suffering of Job, but it was for a great purpose. Another similar example is in the first chapter of Ruth, where because of the death of her husband and two sons, Naomi brought Ruth back with her to her hometown of Bethlehem. The result was Ruth meeting Boaz, and their child was King David's grandfather in the genealogy of Jesus seen in Matthew 1! We also may not see why we are suffering, but God does, and we can trust He has a greater purpose … He knows best!

"DOES GOD EVEN CARE ABOUT MY SUFFERING?"

Maybe a better way to put that question is, "Are we just a pawn for Him to carelessly play with?" I can understand at times we may think that, but God doesn't think that at all. In fact, He allows or causes our suffering out of His unfathomable love for _us_: to better us and to better our relationship with Him. You are more precious to God than you can imagine. From when He created you (Ps. 139:13–16) to what He did through Jesus so you can be close to Him (John 3:16; Rom. 5:8) until you pass on to spend eternity with Him (Ps. 116:15), you are precious. Don't ever forget that … you are _precious_ to Him!

My grandmother, Florence Sprinkle, was the most loving person to me on this earth, and she rarely called me by my name. She always referred to me as "Precious." God is infinitely more loving to me than my Grandma Sprinkle. And He is to you too!

We need to be mature and understand God allows our suffering for a reason. It's pointless to be childish and blame God or attribute to Him what Satan has brought—or what we have brought upon ourselves. Blaming God for something He didn't do or didn't stop is arrogant … and wrong.

Because of Adam and Eve's disobedience, we all have to live in a fallen world where suffering happens. We can't outrun that, but we can run with this: Trust that God will use all our suffering for our good and His glory. Romans 8:28 tells me God will cause all things to work together for good since I love Him, and I am trying my best to love Him and do the right thing. I have lived long enough to honestly say He keeps that promise!

When dealing with some teenage rebellion in our daughter several years ago, someone told us, "Let God write her testimony." Interesting concept, isn't it? It involves trusting God after you stand back up from kneeling in prayer.

"THEN WHY DOESN'T GOD STOP SUFFERING?"

Isaiah 30:20 says, "[T]he Lord gives you the bread of adversity and the water of affliction." That is a striking, eye-opening passage! Bread and water are necessary for life and nutrients for growth. God gives you adversity and affliction because they are necessary for life and are required for your growth. Wow! And when you understand how immensely God loves you and wants what is best for you, going through those hardships is easier knowing they are part of His plan for your growth and better well-being.

Sometimes suffering is the unavoidable consequence of doing something we shouldn't have. Suffering from lung cancer after smoking a pack a day for forty years is dealing with a consequence of bad choices, not externally invoked suffering. Many people quit smoking because they have seen the consequences of doing so. Don't get mad at God if you are suffering the unavoidable consequences of bad choices. However, Jesus said, "I will be with you always," which includes going through those consequences. He didn't have stipulations attached to His promise.

In John chapter 9, we read about Jesus giving sight to a man who was blind from birth. People thought suffering came as a result of sin, either the man's or even his parents. Sometimes it does, basically as a *consequence* of sin. But sometimes suffering is unexplainable except for God's purpose. In verses 2 through 5, Jesus said the man's suffering was so the works of God would be revealed in him. We can learn a great deal from this. We should parlay our suffering into something that "reveals the works of God," or allow Him to, something that glorifies God.

"I DON'T UNDERSTAND WHY I AM SUFFERING; DOES GOD EVEN CARE?"

Sometimes we wonder if He even hears our cries! He does. Psalm 34: 17–19 says, "The righteous cry out, and the LORD hears, and delivers them out of all their troubles. The LORD is near to those who have a broken heart, and saves such as have a contrite spirit. Many are the afflictions of the righteous, but the LORD delivers him out of them all." And Psalm 56:8 says God collects our tears in a bottle. Wow, that is a God who cares and notices and eventually will wipe away all our tears.

"BUT DOES OR WILL GOD HELP US WHEN WE ARE SUFFERING?"

He does and He will … in ways we may not even realize. Sometimes we get "nearsighted" or blinded by our suffering. We just don't see the bigger picture. But God *does*. We need to learn to see outside our suffering and find strength, courage, hope, peace, and even thankfulness.

- Psalm 37:3 says to gain strength and nourishment from God's faithfulness to us.
- Psalm 46:1–3 and 10 tell us to not worry, that we can gain strength from Him and His purposes for us.
- Psalm 55:22 says to cast your burden on Him and He shall sustain you; He shall never permit the righteous (you are righteous by Jesus) to be shaken out of His plan for you.
- Philippians 4:6–9 tells us to not be anxious, but to pray and give it to God. Let His peace, which surpasses understanding, rule in your

heart instead of doubt and fear and worry. Replace bad thoughts with things that are noble, just, pure, lovely, and of good report. Find things to praise God for.

- Philippians 4:7 says to let peace rule and guard your heart and mind like a soldier guards the city, "and the peace of God, which surpasses all understanding, will guard your hearts and minds through Christ Jesus."
- Proverbs 3:5–6 says don't trust your own understanding of things, but trust that what God allows is best for you. He will smooth out the road you are on if you acknowledge Him.

And that is the gist of it: Trust God: He knows and allows what is best for you ... and what will glorify Him.

THE LEGACY OF CHRIS

I have a wonderful story about the connection of suffering and peace as Paul mentioned in Philippians 4:7. And while a connection of those two is certainly attainable, it often does not seem possible to many in the myopic grips of suffering. Many people don't use the terms *suffering* and *peace* in the same sentence, let alone connecting the two. God does, however. So I guess that connection depends on your Christian maturity and your view of God. I know someone mature in Christ, who has the proper view of God: My friend and past coworker Chris Westlake.

Chris suffered (my term, not his) with throat cancer. The ravages of that cancer are saddening, to put it mildly, and it had rendered him unable to eat or talk. I saw him recently, and in a brief conversation, where he "speaks" by writing on a notepad, I came away with a profound realization of the peace we can have through Christ under all circumstances. I also saw first-hand that a person *can* exemplify Philippians 4:7, as mentioned above.

Chris wrote a note to me about bringing glory to God even in his situation. I mentioned I was working on this book, and I would email him a copy of the initial manuscript, as I have a chapter on suffering. He smiled with confident assurance as he grabbed his notepad and wrote these exact words: "I have not experienced suffering. He (God) is covering me in His perfect peace which surpasses understanding and is guarding my heart and mind in Christ Jesus my Lord by grace alone. All Him, none of me."

Peace brings glory to God because of what underlies that peace … trusting a loving, powerful, and gracious God of all comfort. Trust is that unshakable assurance that God knows what is best for you and has your best interests in His confident and capable hands, even though the troubles in this life hit you hard.

A little side note? We often associate suffering with death. Sometimes God may call us to heaven to be with Him to get us out of tough situations here, or maybe He has other reasons. I don't put too much emphasis on that, but it does come to mind. In Genesis 5:24, Enoch and God enjoyed each other so much God just called Enoch up to heaven. Maybe God decided one day it would be a lot easier talking to each other if Enoch came over to God's house. See, I don't think death is as big of a deal to God as it is to most of us.

GOD HAS A DIFFERENT VIEW OF DEATH THAN WE DO.

To God, death is probably like moving from one house to another. To some people, the new house is in the middle of a lake of fire with no air conditioning. To others, it is a mansion by a beautiful stream, with trees, flowers, and air conditioning. It's like God said, "Okay, you've been in that house long enough, time to move to one I have for you." We call it death, but to God, it's moving, thanks to Jesus who overcame death.

The apostle Paul also didn't consider death as a big deal, he called it "falling asleep" (1 Thess. 4:13–18).

Jesus said in John 14:2, "My Father has lots of room for you, and I go to prepare a place for you." Notice He said for *you*, specifically for you with the things *you* like. As you know, Jesus was a carpenter and a builder for about seventeen years prior to His ministry, so when you know Jesus—and He knows you—He knows just what you want in a place you will be living in forever.

Do you *know* the Builder of your new home? Then you will want to go there, and others will be happy for you when you do.

"SO, WHAT SHOULD BE MY RESPONSE TO SUFFERING?"

Our proper response to suffering should be that of trusting Him. Trusting Him is the concept He seems to spend a lot of our years trying to teach us. When we learn that, our suffering seems to get a little easier, a little shorter, and we can have hope. Proverbs 3:5 says to trust God and not ourselves, and Psalm 56, especially verses 3 and 4, says whenever we are afraid, we are to trust God and His Word and not to be afraid. God is bigger and more powerful than any man or any ailment.

Suffering and sorrow go hand in hand. Through those, we wise Christians will "find" ourselves and, ultimately, we find God and become close to Him. Oswald Chambers had this to say in his book *My Utmost for His Highest:*

> We say that there ought to be no sorrow, but there *is* sorrow, and we have to accept and receive ourselves in its fires. If we try to evade sorrow, refusing to deal with it, we are foolish. Sorrow is one of the biggest facts in life, and there is no use in saying it should not be. Sin, sorrow, and suffering *are,* and it is not for us to say that God has made a mistake in allowing them ... You cannot find or receive yourself through success, because you lose your head over pride ... And you cannot receive yourself through the monotony of your daily life, because you give in to complaining. The only way to find yourself is in the fires of sorrow. Why it should be this way is immaterial. The fact is that it is true in the Scriptures and in human experience. You can always recognize who has been through the fires of sorrow and received himself, and you know that you can go to him in your moment of trouble and find that he has plenty of time for you. But if a person has not been through the fires of sorrow, he is apt to be contemptuous, having no respect or time for you, only turning you away. If you will receive yourself in the fires of sorrow, God will make you nourishment for other people.[19]

And that glorifies God, who says, "Call upon Me in the day of trouble; I will deliver you, and you shall glorify Me" (Ps. 50:15).

WHAT ABOUT JOB?

The book of Job is a very disturbing book when you consider it lightly; however, how Job basically maintained trusting God, loving God, and obeying God throughout lends one to conclude it's a book about glorifying God during suffering. And remember, Job did not know *why* the suffering came to him. We do because we are able to read the conversation and challenge in heaven between God and Satan in the first chapter. Job wasn't privy to that.

In Job 42, we see that God called Job His servant, and even though God brought the adversity to Job as stated in verse 11, it says God comforted Job and restored double what he had before … and much more. I think making it through suffering without giving up or giving up on God (or worse) will result in blessings. God loves us and has a purpose for all suffering. With that in mind, you glorify God in your response to suffering … to Him and to others.

It's so comforting to know God knows every detail of your suffering. Second Chronicles 16:9 says, "For the eyes of the LORD run to and fro throughout the whole earth, to show Himself strong on behalf of those whose heart is loyal to Him." Jesus is our strength: He went through more suffering than we ever will, so He understands. The measure of His love for us is found in His suffering.

In Acts 7, we read of the suffering Stephen went through. Hopefully, we never have to go through what Stephen did, but we get a glimpse of the knowledge and compassion from God during our suffering. In verse 56, while being stoned to death, Stephen said, "Look! I see the heavens opened and the Son of Man standing at the right hand of God!" After Jesus died and rose again, He went to heaven and is seated at the right hand of God the Father. However, as we notice in this passage, when Stephen is being stoned, Jesus is standing, as if He *stood up*, wanting so much to help Stephen or to welcome him to heaven. His standing seems to imply, "Oh, Stephen, I know what you're going through. Shortly you will be here with me!"

WHERE TO FIND COMFORT WHEN SUFFERING

"Blessed be the God and Father of our Lord Jesus Christ, the Father of mercies and God of all comfort, who comforts us in all our tribulation, that we may be able to comfort those who are in any trouble, with the comfort with which we ourselves are comforted by God" (2 Cor. 1:3–4).

A pulled pork BBQ sandwich with chili cheese grits and sweet tea, meatloaf with mushroom gravy, chicken fried steak with mashed potatoes and white country gravy over it all, and Oreos dipped in milk. These are my comfort foods, nourishment the physical part of me turns to when I need to "feel better inside." Those are my favorites; what are yours?

Our God is the God of all comfort, and His comfort starts when we read His words in the Bible. That's where the nonphysical part of us turns for nourishment when we need to feel better inside. Numerous psalms are a comfort when we're suffering. Some even tell us what to do during the suffering "season." Notice that in many passages about suffering, God calls it a "season" that will pass as winter season turns to spring and summer. There is comfort right there!

Psalm 41 says we will get strength from God. Psalm 42 tells us to yearn for God. Psalm 63 is one of the best to learn what to do. Look at that treasured psalm and try to pick out from each of the four stanzas what we can do or consider when suffering … and what is the theme of each stanza. Here's a classroom result … hope you can read it:

Romans 8:28 is a "comfort" passage all sufferers can "hang their hat on." I know I have checked my Bible often to make sure it's still there, and it always is. God has proven this passage true to me beyond what I could imagine. And from God's faithfulness to what He promises in that passage, I've gained strength and perseverance through suffering. It has actually become fun to look back and see what He has done. I have hope and confidence with anticipation seeing what He *will* do.

Memorize this verse and say it out loud often: "And we know that all things work together for good to those who love God, to those who are the called according to His purpose."

This is called a conditional promise. It comes true when you have faith it will ("and we know") and when the conditions are met. The promise is God will work out all things for good for you, and the conditions you must meet are that you love God and are called according to His purpose.

The first condition is straightforward and is actually the first and greatest commandment, according to Jesus in Matthew 22:37. Love God. The other condition can be a little elusive or confusing, but it actually isn't. Let me explain.

"Those who are called" is a reference to those people who accepted the calling of Jesus to be saved. Are you a true Christian according to Jesus? Then you fit this condition. Next, "according to His purpose" means according to what God wants to show others. The original Greek word for "purpose" has the same base word as "display" or "show," such as the showbread in the temple. It shows God's great work and provision for everyone to see. To put it in context of this book: God will work all things together for good if you love God and make sure He is glorified.

Now, we cannot end there, because even though God being glorified by working all things out for good is a great end, there is an even greater, more awesome end, because God is just like that: *awesome*!

Romans 8:28 and 29 go together. Verse 29 very eloquently says He also works out those things for good so *you* become more like Jesus! God gets glorified, and you become more like Jesus. Wow! A person may even *want* issues to come up in their life so God is glorified, and they become more like Christ! Maybe not, but that does change the way we look at those tough times in our lives to a little more favorably and not so negatively.

You glorify God not by resorting to sin when suffering comes your way, but by resorting to trusting the *God of all comfort* and learning from Him what He wants you to learn. (So you don't have to go through the "training" again.)

You glorify God by learning about God's character and becoming closer to God during your time of suffering. When you focus on God, and what He is teaching you, the suffering you are going through gets a bit easier … and a bit shorter.

Don't let outside occurrences dictate your theology … God's word does.
—Pastor Dr. Bryan Hughes

PRACTICAL APPLICATIONS

1. Look for God's faithfulness. Start by remembering His faithfulness in and through and after past sufferings.

2. _____

   _____

3. _____

   _____

12 THANKFUL

Being *thankful* to God for all He has done and is doing and will do is not only important but also imperative to bringing glory to God. Also, thank other people when appropriate, and do not be a complainer or grumbler. We live in what I call the age of ingratitude. Entitlement has permeated our society, and, sadly, many Christians. Gratitude or thankfulness needs to make a comeback, and in doing so, we will stand out with a positiveness about us that brings glory to God.

Gratitude toward God should be expressed in saying thanks in every prayer of yours because you glorify God whenever you thank Him for His generosity, faithfulness, love, and mercy. It is also a way to express appreciation for His attributes and character as revealed in His Word. Ramp that up a notch, by expressing gratitude in public, which is a glorious endeavor!

It's one thing to be grateful. It's another to give thanks. Gratitude is what you feel. Thanksgiving is what you do.
—Tim Keller

WORDS OF THANKS ARE ACTION WORDS

Being thankful leads you out of the doldrums or even out of a dark pit such as depression, where your world seems to close in and press you down. Being thankful gets you turned around if you are on a bumpy road in life. Being thankful will sweeten up a sour day.

Be thankful each day—you will be glad you did. Don't wait to be thankful until something good happens or you feel joy; we often do that, and that's backwards. In fact, I will let you in on a little secret ... thankfulness leads to joy and contentment. (More on that later in this chapter.)

You can always find something to be thankful for.
—Fred Brownlee

Be thankful for the material things you have, but especially be thankful for the spiritual things you have. Here's a few to thank God for: salvation, being able to talk to God through prayer, your Bible, being heirs of all God's riches through Christ, Jesus is right now next to God praying for you, Jesus is also preparing a place just for you, the spiritual gift(s) you have been given, meeting Jesus someday, seeing loved ones again in heaven.

When you are feeling down, try one or more of these antidotes to unhappiness:

1. Thank God for a specific situation He has worked out for you.
2. Thank God for something specific He has given you.
3. Thank God for a specific person He has brought into your life.
4. Thank God for a specific time He has been reliable to you, or you have felt His presence.
5. Thank God for something specific you enjoy looking at. Doing so will always pick you, even if just a little.

Being thankful, giving or saying thanks, comes from the word "thanksgiving," which means to be thankful for what has been given to us and is much more than a holiday. When the word "thanksgiving" is used in the

Bible, it's always in the context of praise. When we pray, we are to make our requests known to God *with thanksgiving* (Phil, 4:6), and we are to pray earnestly with vigilant *thanksgiving* (Col. 4:2).

We all have worked hard on something or sacrificed greatly so we can give something special to someone (maybe a Christmas or birthday gift). When we do, and they are not thankful, we are saddened or hurt, and we may even turn away, not wanting to give again. But when that person is thankful, we rejoice inside. We feel really good and want to give again. I think God is the same way. God is glorified when we are thankful, and He wants to do more. So find something, or several things, every day, and thank Him for them.

Gratitude is the attitude that sets the altitude for living.
—James MacDonald

"THANK MY LUCKY STARS!"

"Give proper credit when credit is due" is a saying with much relevance to glorifying God. Being thankful correctly is glorifying to God. By that I mean don't attribute thanks to someone or something not worthy of the thanks. Thank God for the things and blessings He has done to you or for you.

This concept is best described by a couple of quick analogies:

- You didn't notice you ran a red light until another car narrowly missed hitting you, and you say, "Oh thank my lucky stars I didn't get hit!" Really?! God protected you, and you thank some fictitious stars instead of Him?
- The doctor comes into the consulting room at the hospital and tells you the cancer is no longer present in your body, and you thank the doctor and totally forget the God who created that doctor and was gracious and merciful to you.
- You weren't expecting a Christmas bonus since the company you work for is struggling, but you received a bonus anyway, and your response is, "They better have given me a bonus, I work hard for

them!" You're totally forgetting the God who gave you the abilities to do that job and instilling in your boss a sense of generosity toward you. God owns all the money in the world, and you don't even thank Him for some extra!

- You show how unthankful and unappreciative you are of your income by gambling it away hoping to win even more. And then you get angry at God when you don't win big!

- You see someone on the street corner with a sign saying "Car broke down, need help to get to my new job." And you laugh and mumble to yourself, "I'm sure glad I work hard and bought a reliable car." You're totally forgetting God gave you your abilities, your job, and your car, and maybe that person holding the sign neglected to thank God for what they had, so God removed His blessings from them.

- You visit Arches National Park or Zion National Park or the Grand Canyon and marvel at how water created that majestic beauty, completely forgetting the God who created that scenery for you to enjoy nor glorifying Him for His magnificent handiwork. And you don't even credit Him for that water He made.

Isaiah 42:8 says to give God the glory and thanks and praise, not to happenstance or even carved images (anything other than Him). Later in that passage, it says to shout out praises for His handiwork from the mountaintops! Give proper credit to where credit is due, which is God. Period!

THE HISTORY OF GIVING THANKS

The word "thanksgiving" originated in the Bible, where it is used thirty-two times. The word "thank" or "thanks" is there at least another one hundred times.

We actually expect, require, think, or say thanks in any given day over forty times, consciously or subconsciously. The word is so important to daily life that the lack of it is responsible for an estimated 60 percent of relationship conflicts and even divorces. So can you imagine how important it is to give thanks to God?

During a person's troubled times, finding things to be thankful for is the number one "prescription" or advice given by counselors and good friends. It was during our country's most troubled times in 1863 that our president gave this advice and counsel. In fact, he was so adamant that we as a nation pause and be thankful that he signed into law a day to be thankful each year.

THE THANKSGIVING HOLIDAY

Sarah J. Hale wrote a letter to President Lincoln during the American Civil War suggesting that being thankful could unify our nation. In finding things to be thankful for, in the midst of the sins and ravages of war, the president said in a Proclamation on October 3, 1863,

No human counsel hath devised, nor hath any mortal hand worked out these great things. They are the gracious gifts of the Most High God, who while dealing with us in anger for our sins, hath nevertheless remembered mercy. It has seemed to me fit and proper that they should be solemnly, reverently, and gratefully acknowledged as with one heart and one voice by the whole American people. I do, therefore, invite my fellow-citizens in every part of the United States, and also those who are at sea and those who are sojourning in foreign lands, to set apart and observe the last Thursday of November next as a Day of Thanksgiving and Praise to our beneficent Father who dwelleth in the heavens. And I recommend to them that, while offering up the ascriptions justly due to Him for such singular deliverances and blessings, they do also, with humble penitence for our national perverseness and disobedience, commend to His tender care all those who have become widows, orphans, mourners, or sufferers in the lamentable civil strife in which we are unavoidably engaged, and fervently implore the interposition of the almighty hand to heal the wounds of the nation, and to restore it, as soon as may be consistent with the Divine purposes, to the full enjoyment of peace, harmony, tranquility, and union.[20]

Giving thanks is the will of God for you

"Pray without ceasing, give thanks in all circumstances; for this is the will of God in Christ Jesus for you" (1 Thess. 5:17–18).

It is the will of God in Christ Jesus for us to give thanks in everything, and it's tied to praying without ceasing. Isn't it interesting Paul is implying we are to constantly be thankful and even helps us with what to be thankful for … in all circumstances … *everything*. Everything? Really!?

Yes. It helps us to trust God. And doing so brings Him glory.

Psalm 118:1 tells us why we should: "Oh give thanks to the LORD, for he is good; for his steadfast love endures forever!"

And so does 1 Chronicles 16:34: "Oh give thanks to the LORD, for he is good; for his steadfast love endures forever!" So what are the two reasons?

Psalm 107:1 adds another reason; can you spot it? "Oh, give thanks to the LORD, for He is good! For His mercy endures forever."

A very important topic in the Bible

Let's take a look at some passages in the Bible that mention being thankful, see what can be learned, and even recognize some very interesting patterns. I'm not going to put the passages here; I want you to look them up in your own Bible, and write meaningful notes in the margin.

Start it off with one of King David's most famous psalms (songs) that actually isn't in the Old Testament book of Psalms. On one of the most famous days in biblical history, the day the Ark of the Covenant was placed in the Tabernacle, they sang a song … a song of being thankful. David's most important topic when writing songs was to be thankful, and it should be ours too.

It's in 1 Chronicles 16:7–36. Look how it starts off in verse 8. It says we are to do three things. What are they?

1. _____

2. _____

3. _____

You can learn two more things about being thankful from Colossians 3:15 and 17. What are they?

1. _____

2. _____

In addition to being thankful, two other things are required of us in Colossians 4:2. What are they?

_____

_____

We are thankful when we receive gifts. What are the gifts in Ephesians 2:8, James 1:17, John 3:16, and Romans 6:23?

_____

_____

In Philippians 4:6, we are to do a few things with thanks. What are they?

_____

_____

What should be our response to these verses: Psalms 20:4, 28:7, 34:17, and 37:3?

_____

_____

We are to be thankful for what in Psalm 100:4 and Hebrews 4:15–16?

_____

_____

We are to come before God with what three things in Psalm 95:2?

1. _____

2. _____

3. _____

Similarly, in Hebrews 12:28, there are three things tied to worship. What are they?

1. _____

2. _____

3. _____

In 1 Timothy 2:1–3, is Paul telling us to be thankful for unbelievers?

Yes _____

No _____

Turn a few pages, to 1 Timothy 4:4–5. Is it saying we can eat a skunk if we eat it with thanksgiving?

Yes _____

No _____

Second Corinthians 4:15–16 is a wonderful passage about a three-step progression. The third step is to glorify God. What are the first two steps?

1. _____

2. _____

3. To glorify God _____

Second Corinthians 9:11–12 tells about a service we are told to perform that will result in thanksgiving to God. What is it?

_____

_____

CONTENTMENT, THE BRIDGE YOU MUST CROSS

I have underlined passages and written notes in my Bible … a lot. I love God's Word and want to note what is important to me for various reasons. But there is only one verse highlighted in yellow in my Bible, and I didn't do it. My mom did, many years ago. It was obvious it was a very important verse to her, and she evidently wanted it to be important to me.

I was in Texas going to college at the time, a *state* I didn't like very much (compared to western Wyoming and Montana where I grew up and now live). It has come to be a much-needed verse to remember and live by often. It's a verse of trust, thankfulness, and praise: "[F]or I have learned in whatever state I am, to be content: …" (Phil. 4:11).

That verse actually transitions us from thankfulness to praise. Notice Paul said contentment has to be learned: It doesn't come naturally or easy. We have to work at it. I think contentment is a word bridge, a bridge over troubled waters or deep caverns. Sometimes, it's a bridge that can get us from thankfulness to praise. All three work together to bring glory to God.

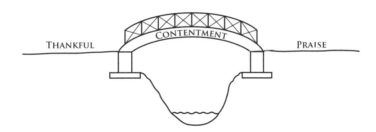

Here is a word picture illustrating how thankfulness becomes genuine praise after we become content, as Paul said. Contentment is also called satisfaction. It is that level of living where you should aspire to live, then hold on to when you get there.

If you are not content with where God has you, or with what God is allowing in your life, you are not trusting Him and you're not thankful, so you're therefore incapable of praising Him.

God is most glorified in us when we are most satisfied with Him in Him.
—John Piper

First Timothy 6:6–12 is a fantastic passage teaching us that godliness with contentment is great gain. All we really need are our basic needs, such as food and clothing, which God promised us in the latter half of Matthew 6. Please study that passage. It will help you to be thankful and content with what God has given you, and then you will praise Him … which glorifies God.

God has promised to supply all our needs. What we don't have now, we don't need now.
—Elizabeth Elliot

THERE'S AN APP FOR THAT

A few years ago, I wanted to improve my thankfulness to God by noting the times God answered specific prayer requests of mine. I looked for an app for my smart phone and found something called a "Thanks Diary." Now, I'm a guy, so the word "diary" didn't appeal to me much, but I downloaded it anyway. A couple of times a week, whenever God answered a specific prayer, I would thank Him and put a reference to that in the Thanks Diary app. I would do so right at the time I thought of it so I wouldn't forget. You see, forgetfulness is the enemy of thankfulness.

After about a month I looked back and saw that a couple of thanks entries a week really started to show me how good God truly is. That was encouraging, so I kept making entries whenever God answered a prayer.

One evening when my mind was filled with ANTs (Automatic Negative Thoughts), I pulled out my phone and looked over the seven or eight months of specific instances of thanking God for His answers to prayers. I was astonished to see this: A couple "thanks" a week turned into several a week, and in the latter few months, there were several "thanks" per *day*!

I came to the evidential realization that the more thankful you are to God, the more He gives you to be thankful for! God loves to do things for thankful people, so He gets glorified!

GOD PLACES DEPOSITS INTO YOUR BANK ACCOUNT.

Psalm 37:3 tells us why we need to keep a "thanks diary." It says to feed on His faithfulness, sort of like how we need to eat food to gain strength and nourishment. You can do that easily when you have quick access to a record of at least some of the times when God was faithful to you, to His Word, or to His promises.

Those specific times of His faithfulness tailored especially for you happened partly so you can use that occurrence of yesterday to help you through your today ... and to give you hope for your tomorrow. You see, Psalm 90:2, Malachi 3:6, Hebrews 13:8, James 1:17, and Revelation 1:8 tell us God is the same yesterday, today, and tomorrow. So how He was faithful yesterday, He will be today. He will be tomorrow too. You can count on that and use His faithfulness that spans time itself as nourishment.

Another way of thinking of this is to "deposit" the times God was faithful to you or to His promises into your "bank account" so you can "withdraw from that account" during a rough time of need.

I can't reiterate enough how important this concept is to a Christian. Being thankful not only acknowledges appreciation to the giver but also is also helpful to you! Remembering how God got you through a rough time or how God honored one or more of His promises or statements in His Word is incredibly helpful, giving you strength and endurance ... and even a peaceful feeling, just like a good meal does. This also brings glory to God.

Remember, be thankful to God for what He has done ... is doing ... and will do.

It is only with gratitude that life becomes rich!
—Dietrich Bonhoeffer

PRACTICAL APPLICATIONS

1. Keep a "Thanks Diary."

2. _____

_____

3. _____

_____

13 PRAISE

We all like to be praised. We like recognition of a job well done. We like to be told our efforts were appreciated, we've done something well, or are enjoyable to be around, and we really like it when someone says so in front of others. God does too.

Conversely, without being praised, a person can fade off into obscurity. God can become obscure to you if you neglect to praise Him.

"ISN'T PRAISE THE SAME AS SAYING THANKS TO GOD?"

Thankfulness, *praise*, and even *worship* have enough similarities they could be linked together as the same. But they are actually different, so much so that they get their own individual label as a way to glorify God in this book.

Merriam Webster's Online Dictionary has these two meanings for the word "praise": (1) to express a favorable judgment of, and (2) to glorify (God or a Saint) especially by the attribution of perfections (excellences).[21]

Isn't the second meaning there interesting in light of this study?! But the first one is very thought provoking as well. It seems to be saying we have judged God and found Him favorable, so the act of praise is expressing that finding.

There are many ways to praise God, and I believe it's highly individualized, as unique as we are unique as a person. I think God likes it that way. We can put our personal touch on our praises to God. It's part of our *relationship* with Him.

Give Him praise when praise is due, and when not due, praise Him then, too.

Why? Because praise is an expression of adoration toward God for who He is and is like, not for what He has done, which is thankfulness. With respect to our God-given volition, God is in control and can even work out the bad things we experience for good (Rom. 8:28), and that is worthy of praise. Being aware of God's gifts and provisions is a great step toward praising Him.

Here is another way of putting it: We are to *thank* Him for what He did (and *didn't* do) and *praise* Him for being wise and loving and generous

We are to praise Him in private, and we are to praise Him in public. I think He is glorified more when we do in front of others.

"Whoever offers praise glorifies Me" (Ps. 50:23).

PRAISE GOD FOR HIS CHARACTER TRAITS YOU RECOGNIZE

I have mentioned several times that Psalm 37:3 says we are to *feed* on His faithfulness. That is a powerful thought, and when we are nourished recalling His good faithfulness in our lives, we always should turn that to praise, because it is recognition of His *character.* And that is what praise is: recognition of God's character traits when we see them ... and even when we don't.

You can thank Him for what He has done for you in the past, what He is doing in your life now, and what He will do for you in the future. You can also praise Him for being the same yesterday, today, and tomorrow. Thank Him for specific answers to prayers; praise Him for not only hearing you but also for answering. Thank God for what He does, and praise Him for who He is.

Thank Him for specific things like your house, your job, your spouse, and for Jesus paying the penalty for your sins. Praise Him for His love, His trustworthiness, His creation we enjoy, for keeping His promises, for the plan He has for your life, and for His Holy Spirit helping and comforting you.

Praising God is one of the best ways to glorify Him. Praise Him for being the immense awesome being who *spoke* the universe into existence out of nothing and still has time to care for, cherish, and deeply love "little ole you."

David wrote most of the psalms, and when reading them you quickly find a pattern of thankfulness and praise. David is thankful for what God does and praises God for who He is … for showing His attributes to David and us all when He chooses. God's faithfulness and His ability to always work things out for good are repeated praises. Psalm 30 is a good example of this, and I love how it ends by glorifying God with praise (and giving thanks, but that is separate): "To the end that my glory may sing praise to You and not be silent. O LORD my God, I will give thanks to You forever" (Ps. 30:12).

Thankfulness and praise are components of worship, both of which glorify God. We'll spend some time studying worship at the end of this book.

JESUS DIDN'T TEACH US TO PRAY WITH THANKFULNESS AND PRAISE.

Here is something to ponder: The Lord's Prayer in Matthew 6:9–13 doesn't have thankfulness or praise in it. Why do you think that is? Your answer just might reveal your level of Christian maturity …

Your life should be a study in praise, and your attitude should be that of thankfulness. Praise and attitude should *not* be relegated to prayer alone.

To some people (and many churches), praise and worship are only expressed through music and singing. That is sad because there are many ways to praise and worship God. However, music probably is the most popular way to praise and worship God, which is okay if we also understand and *practice* the other forms as well.

Music is *not* an okay way to worship God if we are just repeating lyrics on a screen and not considering the meaning of those words and making an effort to express them from our heart. I doubt God is glorified when we read something out loud and not mean it. Or, similarly, we don't really glorify God when we sing something simply because we memorized the words, and when we do, our minds wander elsewhere.

I shy away from lyrics that seem to be overly repetitive. I think when Jesus said in Matthew 6:7 to "not use vain repetitions as the heathen do," song lyrics could be included in the mix because praise or worship music is a form of prayer (communication) with God.

That said, music is a wonderful way to learn about God, worship Him, and praise Him too. We need to realize, however, that not all songs—or even parts of songs—are "praiseworthy." Some songs or lyrics are for us to learn Scripture or biblical concepts, and some are just relating life's situations, neither of which are praise or worship. It's fairly easy to discern the difference. Just look to whom or what the lyrics are directed toward: yourself or people around you ... or God.

We will delve more into how to correctly worship in the last chapter and will include appropriate ways to worship through music.

"IN OUR CHURCH, WE PRAISE GOD THROUGH MUSIC. WHAT IF I CAN'T SING?"

I found over two hundred passages in the Bible relative to praising God, and many of them endorse music as a form of praise. These include Psalm 40:3, Ephesians 5:19, 1 Corinthians 14:26, 2 Samuel 22:50, Psalm 18:49, Colossians 3:16, Acts 16:25, Exodus 15:1, and Revelation 5:9–14.

However, it is a terrible mistake to think we can *only* praise God through music. I used to play several instruments in high school, but thirty-five years later I can barely get a "squeak" out of any of them. I cannot sing either. So does that mean I cannot praise God ... especially in the glorious way He deserves? Of course not!

Thankfully, here are some passages about how we are to praise God that have nothing to do with music or singing:

- Isaiah 63:7 and Deuteronomy 10:21 say we praise God when we verbalize specific examples of God's lovingkindness to us.
- First Peter 4:11 says we praise God when we teach others what we learn from the Bible.
- First Kings 8:56 says we praise God when we tell others specific examples of God keeping His promises.

- First Chronicles 16:28–29 says we praise God when we put money in the offering plate or give Him our time and hard work.
- Daniel 2:20 says we praise God by giving Him the credit in front of authorities.
- Ephesians 1:5 says we praise God by proclaiming His grace to us through Jesus.
- Psalms 111:1 and 150:1 says we are to praise God out loud in church and when we are outdoors in the beauty of His creation. Several passages in 1 and 2 Chronicles say to praise God "standing, with voices loud and high."

Praising God through music does seem to elevate your praise up a notch. Try it! Say out loud, "Praise you Father in heaven for your generosity to me!" Now, say the same thing, but sing it to some made-up melody! It just seems to glorify God a little more, doesn't it?!

I found several passages in Scripture saying David made some instruments to be used specifically to praise God. I think God likes songs with musical instruments when they're directed to Him. We don't want to read into that more than what's there, but it's nice to know someone thought praising God was important enough—and reverent enough—that he made a few instruments specifically designed to praise Him!

"WE ARE TO 'BLESS THE LORD'? ISN'T THAT EGOTISTICAL?"

One of my favorite chapters in the Bible about praising and glorifying God is Psalm 103. However, neither "praise" nor "glorify" are there at all! Quickly read it and notice the word that replaces them:

> Bless the LORD, O my soul; And all that is within me, bless His holy name! Bless the LORD, O my soul, And forget not all His benefits: Who forgives all your iniquities, Who heals all your diseases, Who redeems your life from destruction, Who crowns you with loving-kindness and tender mercies, Who satisfies your mouth with good things, So that your youth is renewed like the eagle's. The LORD executes righteousness And justice for all who are oppressed …

Bless the LORD, you His angels, Who excel in strength, who do His word, Heeding the voice of His word. Bless the LORD, all you His hosts, You ministers of His, who do His pleasure. Bless the LORD, all His works, In all places of His dominion. Bless the LORD, O my soul!

I went to Merriam Webster's Online Dictionary and looked up the word "bless" because I had trouble thinking we could bless the almighty, awesome God! That concept just seemed backward, egotistical, or even just plain *wrong*. But what I learned from Merriam Webster was very informative. One of the meanings of the word "bless" is "to praise, to glorify."[22]

That whole Psalm 130 just bursts with worship when you replacing "bless" with "praise" and "glorify." (Read it aloud that way and see what I mean!!) So, yes, feel free to "bless" the Lord!

Doth not all nature around me praise God? If I were silent, I should be an exception to the universe. Doth not the thunder praise Him as it rolls like drums in the march of the God of armies? Do not the mountains praise Him when the woods upon their summits wave in adoration? Doth not the lightning write His name in letters of fire? Hath not the whole earth a voice? And shall I, can I, silent be?—
—Charles Spurgeon

PRACTICAL APPLICATIONS

1. Praise God for several things during each prayer you pray, especially when praying out loud at dinner or with your friends or family.

2. _____

_____

3. _____

_____

14 GIVING

No topic in the Bible causes more confusion, more frustration, and more misunderstanding than this incredible way to glorify God ... *giving*. There have been deviant people throughout time who have misused giving, misrepresented the requirement of giving, and twisted giving beyond what God says, resulting in a dark light cast on Christians and Christianity.

It saddens my heart when I hear about people turning away from the faith because of their misconceptions about giving. Then there are the preachers who have turned giving into their personal piggy bank, profiteering greedily from wrong teaching about giving, leaving misguided hurt and even destitute people in their wake. Hopefully, this chapter can position giving in its appropriate place ... as a way we can cheerfully glorify God.

Giving includes tithing, freewill giving, and donations, including your time or services. Here is an explanation of each and why they are different:

Tithing is giving to support your local church, mission, and other ministries that further the gospel of Jesus, and enhance His kingdom. ("Kingdom" is defined as believers in Jesus Christ as Lord and King who will one day physically rule the whole earth.) Tithing is a requirement. Genesis 14:19–20 chronicles the first record of tithing; see also Genesis 28:20–22. It became one of the laws of Moses in Leviticus 27:30–34 where everything was established as God's, and 10 percent was to be returned to God. It's sort of like a set tax.

Freewill giving is done above and beyond tithing. An example is when you go to hear a special speaker at your church, and you gift them some money to thank or support them. Again, it is in addition to—not part of—tithing. Freewill giving or offering is voluntary. It can be giving a certain amount you pledged or providing monthly support for a period of time (for a church building project as an example). Leviticus 23:38 lists those different types of giving.

Donating is giving such things as clothing or other items to benefit others. It may also include money and/or your time (such as volunteering to bake cookies for a church group bake sale). Donating your efforts or services, even professional services, counts as well. Serving as an AWANA leader or teaching a Sunday school class are great ways to donate your time and efforts. This is not tithing, and it's different from a freewill gift. It's important to note that donating is also voluntary … but it *should* be done. Acts 20:35 clearly indicates this.

"TITHING SEEMS LIKE PAYING TAXES."

The three types of giving have their origination in the Old Testament, where they were required by law. Tithing to the church in those days was about the same as paying taxes is to us today. For most of the Old Testament period specifically pertaining to God's people, the church was also the government, so the tithe paid for infrastructure, security, and such things as the salaries of the leaders.

It became a little different when Jesus was alive (because the Roman government was in control), yet they let the religious leaders have some power too. That's why, in Matthew 22:21, when Jesus was asked about paying to the government or paying to the church, he asked for a coin and basically said to give both the government and the church their due. In other words, Caesar's image was on the coin, so give to Caesar; God's image is on us, so give to God.

Today, as in New Testament times, paying taxes is required, and so is giving to the church. But the mechanics are a bit different: There isn't a set percentage to give to the church, and we do so not because of law, but because we *want* to. What we find in the Bible about giving is surprisingly overt and can be summed up in this statement: Giving before the time of Christ was a set amount given out of obedience, obligation, and fear. Giving since Christ is an amount you decide out of love, trust, and gratitude.

THE PURPOSES OF GIVING

God knows money is what our society runs on, and the things we purchase are necessary and important to us. That is okay. God also knows money can become more important to us than Him (and our reliance on Him). So He instituted tithing, donating, and freewill giving to help us not put so much emphasis on money and put emphasis on Him.

He also gave us a warning to consider in 1 Timothy 6:10, saying the love of money is the root of all kinds of evil. It doesn't say money is bad, but the *love* of money is … meaning putting too much of a priority on it leads to bad things, including evildoing and a reduction in the joy of life. When your relationship with God is dependent on how much money you have or don't have, something is terribly wrong. Just as money problems are the leading cause of marital problems, money can be the leading cause of your relational troubles with God. Don't let that happen.

So let's get back to the purposes of giving.

God knows there are endeavors He cares about that need funding, and He uses tithing, donations, and freewill giving to fund those. God's plan is brilliant. And if we follow what He says, the church and ministries He cares about are funded, He is glorified, and we are enriched!

There are several reasons to give, all of which bring glory to God:

- It shows we are good stewards of what God gives us.
- It gets us involved in causes God cares about.
- It glorifies God with your possessions.
- Through giving, we obey the tenets of Luke 6:38 and 2 Corinthians 9:7. (So let each one give as he purposes in his heart, not grudgingly or of necessity, for God loves a cheerful giver.)
- It reinforces that giving is to be done systematically (regularly), not by impulse out of emotion or feeling.
- It is to be done the first day of the week (Sunday) (1 Cor. 16:2).
- The amount is what you decide in your heart (2 Cor. 9:7).

Freewill giving, just as in the Old Testament, is done above and beyond the tithe amount you have already decided on (read 2 Corinthians 9:7), and it is another way to glorify God. Many say this type of giving is okay if it arises out of emotion or feeling. Second Corinthians 8:1–4 says it is enabled by God's grace, is encouraged even in difficult times, ends in joy, embodies true Christian living, utilizes the resources you have, excels when done sacrificially, and is a privilege of the true Christian.

Giving *sacrificially* brings glory to God. He is honored much less if you give of your excess, but when you give of what you think you need and trust Him to fill the void your giving created, He is glorified. Remember, God is glorified when you give secretly (Matthew 6:3), because when you give and make sure others know you did, *you* are glorified, not God.

Giving sacrificially also means to give when you don't ever see the results for your giving. You do so out of your love of God and the generosity that produced in your heart. Nothing is expected—you leave the results up to God.

"Is this a contradiction in the Bible?"
Consider these two statements from Jesus: First, he says, "Let your light so shine before men, that they may see your good works and glorify your Father in heaven" (Matt. 5:16).

Then, closely thereafter, he said this:

Take heed that you do not do your charitable deeds before men, to be seen by them. Otherwise you have no reward from your Father in heaven. Therefore, when you do a charitable deed, do not sound a trumpet before you as the hypocrites do in the synagogues and in the streets, that they may have glory from men. Assuredly, I say to you, they have their reward. But when you do a charitable deed, do not let your left hand know what your right hand is doing, that your charitable deed may be in secret; and your Father who sees in secret will Himself reward you openly." (Matt. 6:1–4)

So do those two statements contradict each other? Doing good and giving so others can see versus doing so while no one is looking?

I don't think they contradict, but complement each other. Jesus is referring to a person's *heart* and *motive*. Are you giving so you can be noticed and be praised by people? Or are you giving so God can be glorified, His will gets done, and His ministers and missionaries get paid?

The latter is usually done by a person who doesn't care if they are noticed, because it's not about that or them ... it's about God and His purpose. God may reward you, but that's not why you give at all!

I believe we should never give to get something in return. Doing so serves and glorifies us rather than God. So take that as advice to avoid the so-called "prosperity gospel teaching," model, which seems to expand beyond what the Bible teaches in several areas, one of which is to give so you can get rewarded. Giving to receive a reward is self-centered, not God-centered.

Giving expresses our biblical view of money (God owns it all) and our reliance on Him. It should result in enhancing His kingdom, as Matthew 6:33 teaches. It results in thanksgiving to God and glorifying Him as 2 Corinthians 9:11–12 conveys:

> Now may He who supplies seed to the sower, and bread for food, supply and multiply the seed you have sown and increase the fruits of your righteousness, while you are enriched in everything for all liberality, which causes thanksgiving through us to God. For the administration of this service not only supplies the needs of the saints, but also is abounding through many thanksgivings to God.

So make sure when you give, the focus is on God, not on you. If you are found out and thanked, give God the glory, and even use that as an opportunity to witness for Christ. Your giving should result in God being praised and thanked. Period.

"GIVING IS ..."

Giving is a form of worshipping God: "Give to the LORD, O families of the peoples, give to the LORD glory and strength. Give to the LORD the glory due His name; bring an offering, and come before Him. Oh, worship the LORD in the beauty of holiness!" (1 Chron. 16:28–29).

To expand on giving even further, God knows it is hard for us to give, so He gave us a chapter in the Bible specifically about giving: It's 2 Corinthians 8:1–11. I would suggest you open your Bible to this passage and see for yourself these 11 key points:

1. Giving is enabled by God's grace (v. 1).
2. Giving is encouraged even in difficulty (v. 2).
3. Giving ends in joy (v. 2).
4. Giving must be generous and sincere (v. 2).
5. Giving is done using existing resources, according to your ability (v. 3).
6. Giving excels when done sacrificially (v. 3).
7. Giving must come from a willing heart, not begrudgingly (v. 3).
8. Giving is a privilege and actually a gift from God to do (v. 4).
9. Giving embodies fellowship of believers and true Christian living (v. 4).
10. Giving enables the giver to be a partner of a ministry (v. 4).
11. Giving first involves giving of yourself (dedication), then monetarily, or sacrificially (v. 5).

GIVING IS FOR YOUR OWN GOOD!

The more I studied this topic of giving, the more I came to realize giving is not only to help others and ministries God cares about but is also for our own good too!

God doesn't need or want our gifts and sacrifices, He wants our hearts, but the way to give Him our heart is through gifts. Psalm 50:12–13 quotes God saying just that: "If I were hungry, I would not tell you; for the world is Mine, and all its fullness. Will I eat the flesh of bulls, or drink the blood of goats?" This passage ends with the admonishment to give to Him with thanksgiving, and when it's properly done, it will glorify Him!

But giving is not only for God; giving actually benefits us too!

- God commanded us to give and even says that when you give, there will be a return on your investment, probably in heaven, though it could be during your lifetime here on Earth (see Luke 6:38). I can honestly say my family has been blessed this side of heaven because of giving. Giving shows God's "greatest commandment" to love God and love others.

- Giving causes us to be wise and not foolish during difficult times by keeping a correct relationship with God. This includes trusting Him and His promises, (see Matthew 6:33 where Jesus said God will meet your basic needs if you seek His kingdom and being righteous as He wants).

- Philippians 4:19 is another passage to trust God to honor: "And my God shall supply all your needs according to His riches in glory by Christ Jesus."

- Giving demonstrates you understand God owns everything, and what you *do* have comes from Him.

- You pay your taxes; you also give to your church. Giving funds His work through the church, of which you may have a need for someday. Matthew 22:21 says to give to Caesar what is Caesar's (his image was on the coin Jesus asked for, so He means taxes), and to God what is God's (who's image is on you—see chapter 10).

- Lack of giving robs God and His purposes, as Malachi 3:8–10 teaches. By the way, Malachi 3:10 is not saying to test God and see if He will give you back abundantly if you give. That verse is in the context of the people not tithing to God, resulting in the priest and church workers having to get jobs, greatly diminishing the effectiveness of the church. This caused people to complain. So God said if you give to the church, the church will have an abundant amount for God's purposes.

- Giving according to God's instructions in our New Covenant age we now are in (He tells us how much and when). In 1 Corinthians 16:1–2 we are told to give regularly, on Sunday, saving up if you get paid often, and according to your income.

- Giving funds the church so you have buildings to meet in, and pastors get paid.

- Second Corinthians 9:6 says you will reap according to what you sow (give). If you give little, you will reap little, and vice versa.

- Giving with a cheerful attitude nets these rewards promised in 2 Corinthians 9:6–8:

  1. All grace abounds toward you.
  2. You'll always have all sufficiency in all things.
  3. You'll enjoy abundance for every good work.

- You should always give something. Second Corinthians 9:7 says giving is not a percentage like in the Old Testament, but it is a proportion you know or set … what you purpose in your heart. Second Corinthians 8:3 expands on this, saying the amount you give should be at least based on your ability (you income and means). Even the super-poor widow in Luke 21:1–4 gave according to her ability, so no one can say they can't give.
- Second Corinthians 9:7 also says giving is a privilege, not a duty; you do so cheerfully, not because you have to (grudgingly); and you give because you want to, not because you need to or want something in return (necessity).
- Second Corinthians 9:13 says giving is an act of worship—it will glorify God—which is part of your purpose in life.

When a man becomes a Christian, he becomes industrious, trustworthy and prosperous. Now, if that man when he gets all he can and saves all he can does not give all he can, I have more hope for Judas Iscariot than for that man!
—John Wesley

BE A DO-GOODER

In *addition to* the giving outlined in the previous section, (not *instead of* the above), giving can mean doing good for others. Do you give of your time? Do you help a neighbor out and expect nothing in return?

In Ephesians 6:7, Paul says, "with goodwill doing service, as to the Lord, and not to men." Goodwill means benevolent kindness, and you accomplish it by giving of your time being friendly, helpful, and serving others. Here is a look at each of those with practical applications to giving:

- *Friendly.* When giving of your time, do so with an attitude of kindness toward others and pleasant to be around.
- *Helpful.* Eagerly look for ways to be helpful and things to do that would be. Being helpful puts the needs of others on your radar.
- *Serving others.* Jesus knew when it was good to serve others. Look for ways to remove or reduce the obstacles preventing others from accomplishing their goal or task. Do things for others as a way of giving that will shorten or ease their task.

You may struggle to do that, but do it anyway. How? Paul tells us "with goodwill doing service," linking those three words together (goodwill, doing, and service) which applies to giving of your time and efforts.

In the chapter on love, we talked about the idea of *service* as a way of loving others, and it also applies to giving, which also glorifies God. Both the noun and verb forms of the word apply to serving others as a way of giving:

- Noun: "The action of helping or doing work for someone."[23]
- Verb: "Perform routine maintenance or repair work."[24]

Remember also, Paul insinuates this is hard for us in the Ephesians 6:7 passage because he adds: "as to the Lord, not to men." Giving of your time and efforts to others as if you are doing it for Jesus is like a light shining in the darkness caused by the apathy or abandonment of others who won't give of their time or efforts to help others!

"Let your light so shine before men, that they may see your good works and glorify your Father in heaven" (Matt. 5:16).

"WHEN DOES GOD BLESS A CHEERFUL GIVER?"

I want to reiterate an important statement about giving: God says you will receive blessings when you give, commensurate with your giving, maybe not until you get to heaven, but you will get blessings. I have seen God honor this in my life and my family, with blessings here and now. We have reaped His blessings, and it's directly related to what we have sown (given). It certainly isn't why we give though … and that motive is part of the criteria for God's blessings.

Some (or maybe all) of God's reward blessings may come after we move on to heaven. Our life on this earth—and our life in heaven—are just like moving from one house to another house to God, so we shouldn't think of a division between the two.

Think of this very real possibility: After you move on to heaven, a person comes up to you and gives you a big hug. You didn't know this person on Earth at all, but here they are hugging you. They pull back, holding each side of your face, and with teary eyes look intently into yours and say: "I have to thank you from all that is within me … I am here in heaven due to Jesus, but I would not have the opportunity if it weren't for you writing a check to your church, which used your money to purchase Bibles. I received one of those Bibles while in China … and aside from Jesus, it is because of your giving that I am here. Thank you!" What a blessing that would be.

Here's another important part of the equation. When someone or a ministry does not *accept* giving—or even *ask* for gifts—they are actually depriving the giver of blessings. So if you are legitimately in need, or are a godly ministry, don't be shy to ask or make your needs known. You wouldn't want to deny someone blessings, right? Remember: It's a win-win for you both!

Some people would give if they could feel connected to a need or ministry by doing so. If you have needs, I would suggest writing a list of things your ministry or Christian school or church needs. Someone may pick something on that list, connect with that, and give. And they'll receive blessings they wouldn't have otherwise.

GIVING IS CHEERFUL, NOT BEGRUDGINGLY PAINFUL.
Here are a few one-liners I thought of while researching giving:

- Giving is enabled by grace and is a natural response to grace.
- Giving is an indication of your spiritual maturity.
- Giving is an indication of what you value … your god(s) or God.

- Giving is indicated in your checking account register. It shows what you value most.
- Giving is thanks to God for what Jesus did for us on the cross.
- Giving is an opportunity to enhance or increase Jesus' kingdom.
- Giving indicates your residency—and maybe even your status—in Jesus' kingdom.
- Giving should give you joy, not heartburn.
- When God blesses you, He rarely has just you in mind.

To summarize this section (and the joy of giving), here's a wonderful analogy from Dr. David Jeremiah about giving a big vase of roses to his wife. These written words can't match the eloquence and emotion of hearing him tell it in person, but you should get the gist of it:

> Let's suppose I give my wife a huge bouquet of roses for Valentine's Day. She says, 'Thank you, but you shouldn't have spent the money.' To which I reply, 'Well it's Valentine's Day, and I'm your husband; it's only right because it's my obligation.' She would probably dump the vase of roses on my head.
>
> But if I answer, 'Honey, spending money for you is the joy of my life! I would give you anything I could give you because I love you! I didn't do this because I had to, but because I wanted to because I love you so much!'[25]

You can imagine the two different reactions based on either duty, or heart-felt love. Our love for God outpouring from our heart is the motive for giving.

It's not how much of my money I give God, but how much of God's money I keep for myself.
—R.G. LeTourneau

PRACTICAL APPLICATIONS

1. Tithe regularly and appropriately, and also give to another godly organization you have a connection with.

2. _____

   _____

3. _____

   _____

15 STUDY

Second Corinthians 9:13 says that "while, through the proof of this ministry, they glorify God for the obedience of your confession to the gospel of Christ, and for your liberal sharing with them and all men." This is basically saying you glorify God when you are obedient to your Christianity, studying God's Word and sharing it with others.

STUDYING IS A SURE WAY TO "HEAR" GOD.

God communicates to us when we read the Bible: That is why it's called "God's Word." If you want to actually hear God speak to you, then read the Bible out loud! God may speak to different people in different ways, but reading and studying the Bible is one sure way to hear from Him.

66 books, 40 different authors, and yet, we discover it is an integrated message system from outside our time domain.
—Dr. Chuck Missler

Studying God's Word is always profitable, and it is called His "living Word" because I can honestly say each time I study His Word, there's something I learn that applies directly to some issue I am going through at the time. It seems to be an unending source of help, guidance, and learning.

Over many years of studying the Bible I have also found that not only is following its words the best way to live life to the fullest but we also get to know our creator, what He desires for and from us, and how to discover and realize our purpose in life: To bring glory to God and enjoy Him forever.

The primary purpose of reading the Bible is not to know the Bible but to know God.
—James Merritt

I have known and learned from a lot of very intelligent people in my life. I have listened to them (and others) and read a lot of books by them. I have come to realize that the smartest, most "have it all together" people in the world have one thing in common: they study God's Word and hold it up as the most valuable printed material they own.

THE VALUE OF STUDYING GOD'S WORD

How valuable is God's Word, and why should we study it? Is it relevant to me … *today?* What about all the contradictions and outdated philosophies? Isn't it just a crutch for the simple-minded and naïve? Am I even able to understand the Bible? Isn't it too huge and daunting? Those are very good and very common questions and will be answered fully to your complete satisfaction in this chapter. I know, because I used to ask them too …

In chapter 7, we learned that Proverbs 22:1 says a good name is to be chosen over riches and is more valuable than silver or gold. Do you think God has a good name? I certainly do, especially the name of Jesus. But do you know there is something more valuable than His name? One of the greatest kings to ever live said in Psalm 138:2: "For You have magnified Your word above all Your name." God values His Word (the Bible) above His name!

You should too.

Reading the Bible will help you get to know the word, but it's when you put it down and live your life that you get to know the author.
—Steve Maraboli, *Life, the Truth, and Being Free*

Silver, gold, and fine rubies are very valuable. However, the wisest man to ever live, Solomon, said there is something more valuable than those ... wisdom, as gained from the Bible: "Happy is the man who finds wisdom, And the man who gains understanding; for her (wisdom's) proceeds are better than the profits of silver, and her gain than fine gold. She is more precious than rubies, and all the things you may desire cannot compare with her" (Prov. 3:13–15).

Knowledge and wisdom are similar, but very different. You turn one into the other with some effort. Knowledge is knowing things; wisdom is how to apply those things to your life. You use knowledge from the Bible to change your life.

James says to not be deceived into thinking you are okay. Most people aren't "okay" in relation to what the Bible says; in fact, they need the Bible to improve and to be "doers" of the Word, not just "hearers" only: "But be doers of the word, and not hearers only, deceiving yourselves" (James 1:22).

We have help when we study the Bible. The Holy Spirit is in each of us true Christians, and part of His purpose is to *illuminate* the Scripture for us (see John 14:26). The Bible seems living because you can read a certain passage several times over the years, and each time it seems to be a little bit different than the previous time but is directly to the point of what you need to hear at the time.

Develop a *love* for reading His Word. Set a time each day to read it, just as you have set times each day for eating or showering. God's Word is the "bread of life" (John 6:35), and we are cleansed by the "washing of water by the word" (Eph. 5:26).

Sow a thought and you reap an act; sow an act and you reap a habit; sow a habit and you reap a character; sow a character and you reap a destiny.
—Ralph Waldo Emerson

Make it a habit to study your Bible. A ritual is a ruler, and you want your life ruled by God's Word. Remember, Erasmus said, "It takes another nail to drive out a nail." And you *can* correct a bad habit by forming a new one, one that includes prayer and Bible reading.

I know, studying God's word can be difficult for many of you. Some of you may find it boring or a chore. A few of you may not even get much out of the Bible; others find it very hard to sit down and read any of it. Let me say this: I was there. I can relate wholeheartedly. But I overcame all that and am *so* happy I did. You can too.

I realized all the excuses not to read the Bible came from Satan. The Holy Spirit in every Christian instills a desire and love for reading the Bible, but Satan does not want you to read it, so he hits you with every excuse until one sticks, and you walk away. Whom do you serve then? God's Holy Spirit or Satan?

So buck up and overcome Satan. You have the power.

I also know how much hope comes from reading and studying the Bible. A few years ago, I heard professional baseball pitcher Dave Dravecky speak about the devastating effects of cancer and issues with his pitching arm, and he mentioned his favorite Bible verse. It's a good one, too, as hope is its focus: "For whatever things were written before were written for our learning, that we through the patience and comfort of the Scriptures might have hope" (Rom. 15:4).

PRACTICAL ADVICE FOR STUDYING GOD'S WORD

These tips helped me to get into the Word and enjoy it. I hope they will help you too:

- Just read a paragraph, unless you want to read more. Don't make reading the Bible daunting.
- Look for a word in each sentence that jumps out at you, and dwell on that word and its implication to the passage. Usually, it's a verb, but many times it's not. The Holy Spirit is usually trying to teach you something by zeroing in on just one word.
- Selah. You see that in the Psalms, but it's applicable anywhere in Scripture. It means "pause and think about that." So *do* that. Read something, and sit back and ask yourself, "What does that mean to me and my life?"
- The Bible is huge, so you don't have to read it all. Don't gasp at that: I am just saying the Bible is meant to be read in bite-sized pieces, a little at a time.

- Read what interests you. Usually, New Testament books are better to read and apply to your life more readily than Old Testament books. I would suggest reading the last three chapters in Ephesians … they may just transform your life!
- Read a couple of sentences from the book of Proverbs often. It's written by the wisest man who lived, so there's lots to learn there.
- Read a passage until you get something out of it, then pause and ask how you can apply that to your life today.
- Try to remember what you read later in the day or the next day. Make it a game if you need to, and give yourself points if you can remember what you read.
- Memorize Scripture verses. Yes, people still do that, and so should you!
- Pray that God will teach you something and show you a passage you need. He will!
- Write down what you read, and learned. We retain 80 percent more if we write it down, only 20 percent if we don't, so improve your chances of remembering … write something down in a journal, or just take some notes.
- Regularly attend a small-group Bible study. It is amazing how the camaraderie of others and their viewpoints of Scripture can help you learn the Bible.
- Look for how the passage you read applies to Jesus or your relationship with Him, or how to treat others as Jesus would. The Bible, as a whole, points to Jesus, so what you just read might in some way or another.

You know, in thinking about that last point, the Bible testifies of Jesus. He is the reason you read: to get to know Him and be like Him (1 Pet. 2:21), to have an abundant life through Him (John 10:10), to get power and grace from Him (2 Cor. 12:9), love like Him (John 3:16 and 1 John 4:16), and to enjoy peace (John 14:27), joy (John 15:11), rest (Matt. 11:28), and eternal life (Rom. 6:23) with Him in heaven (Matt. 25:31 and Rev. 21:4)! Why would you *not* want any of these?!

"BUT AREN'T THERE CONTRADICTIONS AND ERRORS IN THE BIBLE? CAN IT STILL BE TRUSTED?"

The Bible is the infallible Word of God. There are no contradictions. Those who say there are have not studied it, or they would know there are none. God's Word has been divinely preserved and kept accurate throughout time. It has also been validated by secular historians and actual writings recently found. Verifications are too numerous to count. God's Word has been preserved ... and you can wholly trust it.

If you have any doubts about the reliability of the Bible in a reputable translation, I would suggest this short, well-done free booklet you can even read online: gty.org/library/articles/45TRUST/you-can-trust-the-bible. Or, view this YouTube video: youtube.com/watch?v=z9PAX-2ZABk.

I love how Paul taught Timothy to trust the Word of God and its uses in 2 Timothy 3:16–17: "All Scripture is given by inspiration of God [Literally God-breathed], and is profitable for doctrine, for reproof, for correction, for instruction in righteousness, that the man of God may be complete, thoroughly equipped for every good work."

God's truth, the Bible, is divine revelation, not human intuition. One doesn't have to be very bright to choose which to believe. I am always amazed at how gullible some people are, choosing to believe what fallible people say over what *the* infallible God says. Romans 1:22 tells of those fly-by-night orators: "Professing to be wise, they became fools."

The Bible is the inevitable outcome of God's continuous speech. It is the infallible declaration of His mind.
—A. W. Tozer

"STUDY SOUNDS HARD. I'LL NEED SOME HELP."

Study means more than reading God's Word. It means to search the passages and review related or parallel passages. I like to use what I call the "two or three witness" rule when studying the Bible. It comes from Matthew 18:16 and 2 Corinthians 13:1: "By the mouth of two or three witnesses shall every word be established." I think every principal passage in the Bible has that same principle repeated two or three other places in the Bible. I try to find them and see what the context is in those places.

Similarly, I like to use Scripture to *explain* Scripture. A good example of this is in the study of the book of Revelation. The explanation of all the idioms found there (locusts, a ram, fiery coal, a dragon, a lampstand, and so on.) are in the Old Testament. In fact, you go to nearly every Old Testament book in the Bible to get explanations for things in Revelation. Isn't that brilliant by the Holy Spirit?! Another example of using the Bible to explain the Bible is referencing Mark 2:7 to explain why the high priest tore his clothes and accused Jesus of "blasphemy" in Matthew 26:65.

I also like to use a good commentary from a reputable group or pastor (I personally use Dr. John MacArthur's numerous commentaries and the *MacArthur Study Bible*), a good Bible dictionary, and a concordance such as Vine's or Strong's to enhance and aid my study.

Today's internet or Google searches can be quick and helpful, but they may also be like "walking among land mines" due to errant or heretical sites. Reputable ones will post their statement of faith, which can be informative if you know what to look for. Satan is on the internet too, so try to stick to reputable sources such as www.biblestudytools.com, www.openbible.info, www.biblegateway.com, www.blueletterbible.org, or www.gty.org

Use tools to help you study God's Word. In this electronic age, they are easily accessible and quick. Most of us can be a "Bible scholar" compared to just forty years ago. Even Google is very helpful if you use discernment. On my smart phone, I use the YouVersion Bible app. On my computer, I use eSword at www.esword.net. Most of these resources are free; some notable downloads and Bible versions are available at a nominal cost. Logos Bible Software at www.logos.com is incredible but costly. If you would like to donate or freewill gift it to me so I can purchase it, please let me know …

WHAT YOU GET WHEN YOU STUDY THE BIBLE

What do you get from studying God's Word?

- *Help in understanding it.* Second Timothy 2:7 says, "Consider what I say, and may the Lord give you understanding in all things." Also consider John 16:13: "[W]hen he, the Spirit of truth, comes, he will guide you into all the truth."
- *Faith.* See Romans 10:17: "So then faith comes by hearing, and hearing by the word of God."
- *Guidance.* Psalm 119:105 says, "Your word is a lamp to my feet, and a light to my path.
- *A better relationship with Jesus.* The Bible points to Jesus, as seen in John 5:39: "You search the Scriptures, for in them you think you have eternal life; and these are they which testify of Me."
- *Nourishment and growth.* First Peter 2:2 says, "Like newborn babes, long for the pure milk of the word, so that by it you may grow in respect to salvation."
- *Inspiration, training, correction, and instruction.* See 2 Timothy 3:16–17: "All Scripture is given by inspiration of God [literally God-breathed], and is profitable for doctrine, for reproof, for correction, for instruction in righteousness, that the man of God may be complete, thoroughly equipped for every good work."
- *Warning.* Psalm 19:11 admonishes, "Moreover, by them Your servant is warned; in keeping them there is great reward."
- *Restoration.* Psalm 19:7 says, "The law of the LORD is perfect, restoring the soul."
- *Wisdom, knowledge, and understanding.* We learn this in Proverbs 2:6: "For the Lord gives wisdom; from His mouth come knowledge and understanding." Psalm 19:7 adds: "The testimony of the LORD is sure, making wise the simple."
- *Judgment and guidance.* Hebrews 4:12 advises, "For the word of God is living and active and sharper than any two-edged sword, and piercing as far as the division of soul and spirit, of both joints and marrow, and able to judge the thoughts and intentions of the heart."

- *Accomplishment.* See Isaiah 55:11: "So will My word be which goes forth from My mouth; it will not return to Me empty, without accomplishing what I desire, and without succeeding in the matter for which I sent it."
- *Freedom.* John 8:31–32 tells us, "So Jesus therefore was saying to those Jews who had believed Him, 'If you continue in My word, then you are truly disciples of Mine; and you will know the truth, and the truth will make you free.'"
- *Sanctification and truth.* We find this in John 17:17: "Sanctify them in the truth; Your word is truth."
- *Protection from sin.* Psalm 119:11 tells us: "Your word I have hidden in my heart, that I might not sin against You."
- *Discernment.* Leviticus 10:10 reminds us: "so as to make a distinction between the holy and the profane, and between the unclean and the clean …" See also Hebrews 5:14, Psalm 119:66, and Philippians 1:9–10.
- *Peace.* Read Psalm 119:165: "Great peace have those who love Your law [Bible], and nothing causes them to stumble."
- *Strength.* Joshua 1:7 tells us, "Only be strong and very courageous, that you may observe to do according to all the law." See also Psalm 31:24, Psalm 34:19, Psalm 112:7, and Philippians 4:13.
- *Stabilization.* In Psalm 1:3, we read: "He will be like a tree firmly planted by streams of water, which yields its fruit in its season and its leaf does not wither; and in whatever he does, he prospers."
- *Success.* Joshua 1:8–9 explains: "This book of the law shall not depart from your mouth, but you shall meditate on it day and night, so that you may be careful to do according to all that is written in it; for then you will make your way prosperous, and then you will have success. Have I not commanded you? Be strong and courageous! Do not tremble or be dismayed, for the LORD your God is with you wherever you go."

My wife was in the banking business as a teller line supervisor. She would train her tellers how to recognize counterfeit money by having them intently study *real* money. Once they knew what the real thing looked and felt like, it was easy to spot the counterfeit. That is a great analogy for studying the true Word of God. It will enable us to recognize other publications or reports that are fake, even if it is just a few words that are not right.

Another reason for studying the Bible is found in 2 Timothy 3, where Paul tells young Timothy that perilous times will come and lists the traits of people we see so prevalent today—people will be lovers of themselves, lovers of money, unthankful, unloving, slanderers, lovers of pleasure rather than lovers of God, despisers of good, and so on.. How do you not become one of those "Facebook Flamers"? How do you not fall into their traps and be "deceived by those evil people and impostors who grow worse and worse, deceiving and being deceived"?

Well, Paul says you *must* continue in studying God's Word and those things that you learned from faithful teachers from childhood. They will make you wise, complete, and thoroughly equipped for every good work. Read parts of the Bible daily and let it dwell in you richly. Read faithful books and listen to faithful teachers through your church, podcasts, even YouTube. Being faithful is the key. Faithful means holding true to what God's Word says.

JOIN THE NOBLE ELITE.

Kings and people of nobility study the Scriptures. You can be both!

Proverbs 25:2 says, "It is the glory of God to conceal a matter, But the glory of kings is to search out a matter." This is an interesting verse … what do *you* think it means? I don't think God hides main gospel truth so only a few can find it, but this indicates there are some special things you can learn when you study (meaning to search out a matter) the Bible. The book of Revelation starts out by saying there is a special blessing when you study that book. Be like a king, and get special blessings … they're waiting for you when you study Scripture!

Acts 17:10–12 says, "The brothers immediately sent Paul and Silas away by night to Berea, and when they arrived they went into the Jewish syna-gogue. Now these Jews were more noble than those in Thessalonica; they received the word with all eagerness, examining [searched or studied] the Scriptures daily to see if these things were so. Many of them therefore believed, with not a few Greek women of high standing as well as men." Why is what they did necessary? They didn't want to blindly take any person's spoken or written words as "gospel truth" without first consulting the Bible to verify what they said. Noble people verify. Ronald Reagan was famous for saying "Trust, but verify," which readily applies here.

How to study the Bible

Paul told Timothy in 2 Timothy 2:15 to study God's Word diligently, so don't be ashamed to do so *or* be ashamed to use God's word when talking to people. He said, "Be diligent to present yourself approved to God, a worker who does not need to be ashamed, rightly dividing the word of truth."

One of the suggestions I gave earlier to help you study the Bible is to find a word or two in each passage that jumps out at you and zero in on it. I call them "*bam!*" words. Here are two *bam!* words from that previous passage:

The word "diligent" means to study meticulously. Several versions of the Bible use the word "study," but it is far deeper than that. The Greek word also means to develop a love for, for wanting all there is … sort of like studying a very famous painting you love or going to every single football practice because you love the game and want to learn all you can about it and become good at it. Diligent … *bam!*

Remember: God wants you to be diligent, and it also glorifies God. Moses said in Deuteronomy 6:17, "You shall diligently keep the commandments of the LORD your God." He adds to that in Deuteronomy 28:1: "If you diligently obey the voice of the LORD your God … the LORD your God will set you high above all nations of the earth." Both passages refer to the Bible and the need to study it.

The other example is *dividing*, which means to correctly dissect, or to separate into parts, and to study those parts and how they combine to make the whole. The Bible is meant to be studied intently, even individual sentences and individual words, and then related to the segment in its entirely. The Bible is the only document where the author (God) is so confident in the wording, He tells us to not be ashamed to work hard to study it, even word by word … one at a time if you want. Rightly dividing … *bam!* Give it a try: you will be amazed!

Many passages in Scripture help us grow and mature as a Christian. The four Gospels can be viewed, especially when studying Jesus, regarding how He reacted to different groups of people or situation at hand. The Psalms and Proverbs are great for helping us grow, and other books in the New Testament, such as Galatians, Ephesians, James, Philippians, and 1 Peter are equally nourishing to our spiritual development.

Whatever you are studying in Scripture to try to live a more biblical life—more like Jesus—try to use the STEPP process:

- *Subject.* What is the subject of the passage, or the main character?
- *Topic.* What is the main topic being conveyed?
- *Examples.* What are the examples, analogies, parables, illustrations, or other insights used to make the subject and topic more understandable to you?
- *Principles.* After figuring out the first three, you can probably arrive at the main principles the passage conveys. Identify what it is, or what they are, and listen for the teaching of the Holy Spirit. Pray for understanding of the passage (which the Holy Spirit will help you with) and the implications for your life.
- *Practical application.* How can you make a real change in your life by applying these principles? These could include a course correction to make, a habit to stop (or form), a truth to believe, or an example to imitate.

If it helps, I would suggest taking a passage and writing down three key points related to that passage. This is a great way to learn from the Holy Spirit who helps you understand Scripture! I like to use three points (partly because God exists in three) because it's easy to come up with that many in a short period of time, and we tend to remember three examples more readily than many more.

LOCATION, LOCATION, LOCATION

The three most important things in real estate ("location, location, location"[26]) applies to studying the Bible too. Here is what I mean:

First location: When considering a verse, it is very important to get the verse correct by understanding its *context*. Learn the *context of the verse* or passage by considering what book in the Bible it is from and how it relates it to the whole of that book. You should also read several verses before, and several after, to get an idea of the context. For example, if you pulled out this sentence from a book: "Bob was standing at the bank," you need to read before and after to find out if Bob was fishing by a river or depositing his paycheck.

Second location: The *context of the period* or place and time the passage occurred is extremely helpful when studying a passage. This can make the passage shine with meaning, relevance, and emphasis. For example, consider John 8:12, when Jesus said, "I am the light of the world. He who follows Me shall not walk in darkness, but have the light of life." Jesus said this in the outer courtyard of the temple in Jerusalem where they had just extinguished the huge menorah during a festival celebrating the pillar of fire that lit the way for the Israelites out of Egypt. Knowing that menorah lit up the whole area adds wonderful meaning, and it is especially impactful when you understand Jesus was also equating Himself to that light in the wilderness.

Third location: Think about the *context of your life*. How does the passage apply to what is going on in your life at the time? For example, Psalm 37 is especially helpful when you are troubled, discouraged, angry or upset with others, and distraught. Psalm 131 is equally helpful when you are stressed. Ephesians 4, 5, and 6 tells you how to live in our harsh world and deal with the people around you.

INTERESTING OBSERVATIONS

Here are some of my observations in learning to study the Bible:

- Unbelievers have trouble studying and understanding the Bible. 2 Corinthians 2:14, John 1:5, Matthew 13:13, and Isaiah 44:18 are good examples. Many people tend to "not get it" or "get it wrong."
- Jesus expects us to study the Bible. Many times, when someone would ask Him a question, he would answer, "Have you not read …?" So don't let Jesus down, read your Bible … your questions will be far fewer.

- It takes faith to study the Bible, and when God sees your faith, He will help you understand even more. (See Hebrews 11:1, 3, and 6.)
- God rewards Christians who diligently study the Bible. (See Hebrews 11:6, Revelation 1:3.)
- Make time to study—20 minutes at the very least—and be sure it's uninterrupted study. Get in the zone!
- Before reading one of the books in the Bible, read an overview of the book, author, date, and some period information first. A good study Bible should provide this in the preface before each book.
- The Old Testament (other than Proverbs and pPsalms) is generally meant to read as a narrative. It's kind of like reading a novel.
- The four Gospels are about Jesus from four different points of view. It's fun to learn about each writer (Matthew, Mark, Luke, or John) and understand his perspective prior to reading his Gospel.
- Revelation is all about Jesus … and what's coming. There are several different timelines, which can be hard to keep straight, but you can do it since many movies today are constructed in much the same manner. Studying Revelation will take you to nearly every Old Testament book to figure it out. It is the only book that promises a special blessing to those who study it (Rev. 1:3).
- The rest of the New Testament is meant to be read in small parts, studying those parts, and then asking, "How can I apply this to my life?" Most of it isn't really written *to* us, but is certainly written *for* us.
- Pick a book and master it. Become an expert in that book. I would suggest James, Philippians, or Colossians; they are very useful to daily living. Teach that book to others.
- Read a book over and over and over again. The best way to learn something is repetitiveness (Isa. 28:10).
- Pray before and during your reading. Read it as if it's a letter given to you by the author and the author is sitting right next to you while you read it asking, "So, what do you think?"
- Write in your Bible. Underline away, take notes, and make references to other passages. Just *write* … it's okay!

- Write down things you don't understand, and ask God to help you understand them … in His time. Write down the date of your request, because at some point, you will probably understand the passage and glorify God when you do!
- Recall what you read later in the day. Remembering helps you learn.
- Read with the mindset of "what can I learn, and apply to my life?" Then listen to that still, small voice—the Holy Spirit—who illuminates Scripture.
- Read a passage until something really "speaks to you." Then read it several times and Selah (which means to pause and think about that).
- Ask yourself "What does this passage say?" more than "What does it mean to me?"
- Use the principle of the Trivium. (This involves grammar, logic, and rhetoric.) Read the passage you are studying. Then sit back and think about it and ask yourself what it means. Finally, explain it out loud. Try it … it really helps!
- Pick a Bible version and stick with it. If you want my advice as to which one, use the one your main teaching pastor preaches from. I also like one that's been around a while, and will continue to be, so when you memorize verses, it's relevant for your whole life. I personally use The New King James version, partly for the reasons outlined above.

DON'T BELIEVE THESE LIES

Man's mind is so formed that it is far more susceptible to falsehood than to truth.
—Desiderius Erasmus

We need to read God's truth, the Bible, often because we need to be reminded of truth. Truth is a staunch, stalwart, immovable, and impenetrable reality, but it can get mud and dirt on it, making it hard to see. We have to study God's Word *regularly* to clean the dirt off and see the glorious majestic truth again.

Satan is called the Great Deceiver and the Father of Lies, as he well knows we tend to "fall" for his deceptions. Since he doesn't want you in God's Word, here are some of his common lies about the Bible:

Reading the Bible is a chore.	Reading the Bible is too daunting.
You won't understand it.	Only trained theologians can understand it.
It's too overwhelming.	It's full of violence, killing, racism, and prejudice.
It takes too long.	You can make it say whatever you want.
There are contradictions in the Bible.	It's a crutch for weak people.
You can't take it literally.	It contradicts science, so it can't be trusted.
The Bible is old and not relevant today.	It's anti-women. It's intolerant. It's hateful.
You can't trust it, it's changed over time.	It's just fairy tales and fictitious.
There are better books than the Bible.	It's boooooring.
It's only a history book.	You don't need it.

When reading that list, you will notice those allegations that attack God. They only prey on our human weaknesses. They also can cause doubt ... doubt about the validity of the Bible and doubt that you can gain anything from it. A very similar tactic was used by Satan to cause Eve to sin by eating from the forbidden tree in Genesis 3:1–5.

Don't let Satan put doubts about God's Word in your thoughts, and don't let anyone else do it either! Any doubt or any negative thoughts or conceptions should be stopped as lies at your door. Don't entertain lies. They are a waste of time, keep you from studying His Word, and only lead down a bumpy, rocky potholed road full of darkness and despair. Hope and life is found in God's Word, and so is bringing glory to Him.

Incredibly wonderful things done for the betterment of our civilization and glory to God start and continue with studying God's Word. Satan doesn't want this to be a wonderful world, so you have a choice: a wonderful and joyous world of love and hope to live in or a crappy world of hate and despair. The choice depends on how God's Word is factored into the equation. There is power in God's Word (Heb. 4:12; Rom. 1:16). How you choose to accept that—and what you do with it—can either bring glory to God ... or not.

You Christians look after a document containing enough dynamite to blow all civilization to pieces, turn the world upside down and bring peace to a battle-torn planet. But you treat it as though it is nothing more than a piece of literature.
—Mahatma Gandhi

It *is* more than a piece of literature. It is the very breathed-out words of *the* God. The One, the I Am, the LORD God, the creator and sustainer of everything. He wrote this book and wants you to read it, study it, quote it, and make it part of your everyday conversations.

Have you ever been in a conversation with others and someone quotes a friend of yours? That brings validity to the conversation and honor to the quoted person. God likes that and is glorified when we quote His words too.

God is glorified when we study His Word, obey what He says, rely on what He says, let what He says change and improve our life, and pass along to others what His Word says. And this brings us to the last way to glorify God in the next chapter.

PRACTICAL APPLICATIONS

1. Set a specific time to study God's Word each day ... even if just for 20 minutes.

2. _____

   _____

3. _____

   _____

16 TEACH

When seeds are planted, a crop is expected to be produced, from which others are fed. This analogy holds true to the planting of God's Word in you and what He has done in you. What you have learned (including the impacts His Word has made in your life) needs to be shared with others for their growth and enhancement.

Teaching or sharing God's Word to others clearly and accurately brings glory to God. Whether you teach God's Word to your family, friends, lead a small group Bible study, or teach Sunday school, you honor and glorify God when you do.

> You shall love the LORD your God with all your heart, with all your soul, and with all your strength. And these words which I command you today shall be in your heart. You shall teach them diligently to your children, and shall talk of them when you sit in your house, when you walk by the way, when you lie down, and when you rise up. You shall bind them as a sign on your hand, and they shall be as frontlets between your eyes. You shall write them on the doorposts of your house and on your gates. (Deut. 6:5–9)

The greatest way to learn something is to teach it. In Titus 2:1,[27] Paul tells Titus to "teach what accords with sound doctrine" (ESV). And the word "sound" is significant. According to the Merriam Webster Online Dictionary, "sound" means: "free from injury or disease, free from flaw, defect, or decay, free from error, fallacy, or misapprehension <sound reasoning> exhibiting or based on thorough knowledge and experience, legally valid, logically valid and having true premises, agreeing with accepted views, showing good judgment or sense."[28]

With that meaning in mind, you can see why Paul expects Titus and, by extension, us to use and teach from the only collection of writings that explicitly fulfills that meaning … God's Word, the Bible.

WISE PEOPLE LEARN TRUTH, THEN THEY TEACH IT TO OTHERS.

God's Word is truth. It is accurate and solid—truth that is truly true. God said so in Isaiah 45:19: "I, the Lord, speak the truth." And God's Son Jesus, when praying for His disciples and for us in John 17:17, said exactly that: "Sanctify them by Your truth. Your word is truth." Wise people say so also. Here is one of my favorites:

The inerrancy of Scripture is the foundational doctrine in which all other doctrines rest, and the Psalmist rightly said, 'If the foundation be destroyed, then what can the righteous do?'
—Norman Geisler

Considering what wise people say about the Bible; the wisest man to ever live was a very godly and biblically knowledgeable man who studied the Scriptures. He did stray away from being obedient to God, however, and delved into all the worldly things he could. But just before he died, Solomon thought over his life, and realized two important things he wanted to share with everyone before his death. They're found in the last chapter of Ecclesiastes. To preface his comments,

- There are a lot of books out there, and it's wearisome reading them, but one book alone has scholarly truth, wisdom, and admonishment: it is God's Word, the Bible.

- After he carefully considered everything in his life ... most of which he considered vanity, he penned these words: "Let us hear the conclusion of the whole matter: Fear God and keep His commandments, for this is man's all. For God will bring every work into judgment, including every secret thing, whether good or evil" (Eccles. 12:13–14).

Solomon was *not* saying to read the Bible and only the Bible, but he was saying there are many good books to read and teach—and you should—but one is the best: the Bible. So make sure the Bible is top of your list. You won't grow weary reading it, so do and keep what it says. Honor, respect, and revere God in all you do.

"Not unto us, O LORD, not unto us, But to Your name give glory, Because of Your mercy, Because of Your truth" (Ps. 115:1).

"BUT I'M NOT A TEACHER!" "OH YES, YOU ARE!"

God's plan for you is to teach His Word to others, which glorifies Him. You are an influence on other people, so make your influence something from God's Word. Jesus, in Matthew 18–**20**, commanded us to teach others just minutes before He went to heaven. As such, it is His last great requirement for us: To make disciples and teach them. A disciple is literally a personal follower of Jesus, someone you teach to follow Him and teach what Jesus said. You are to find someone, or some people, and teach them.

Paul told the people in the church at Colossae to teach everyone the gospel of Jesus: "Him we preach, warning every man and teaching every man in all wisdom, that we may present every man perfect in Christ Jesus."

I heard this interesting and provocative description from a pastor friend of mine: Charley Carpenter said if each of us teaches at least one person, makes at least one disciple, and then each of those do the same, within about thirty-six years, everyone on the earth would be disciples of Jesus. So what part of this is your responsibility? Teaching at least one person about Jesus and to follow Jesus. It takes time and intentional effort. But what a *glorious endeavor!*

Second Timothy 2:2 says, "And what you have heard from me in the presence of many witnesses entrust to faithful men who will be able to teach others also." You are one of the "faithful" Paul mentions here. What God has taught you through His Word, pastors, teachers, and/or mentors, you are to pass on to others.

I think the pattern in Scripture is to be mentored by someone and to mentor someone. So it's wise to always be learning the Bible from someone (like a pastor or a godly friend) and to teach someone (like your children or a friend or others in a small-group Bible study). Jesus told us to mentor someone in Matthew 28:19–20, where he said to teach others what He taught.

This "pass through" is a responsibility you have. We are not put here to just eat and be entertained; we are to do good works that build or enhance the kingdom of Jesus (Matt. 6:33), which includes teaching people as Jesus commanded: "Go therefore and make disciples of all the nations, baptizing them in the name of the Father and of the Son and of the Holy Spirit, teaching them to observe all things that I have commanded you; and lo, I am with you always, even to the end of the age" (Matt. 28:19–20).

To teach others, we need to lay a foundation, which we do by stating what, why, and how. Paul gives the first two in this foundational passage: "All Scripture is breathed out by God and profitable for teaching, for reproof, for correction, and for training in righteousness, that the man of God may be competent, equipped for every good work" (2 Tim. 3:16–17 ESV).

Invest in other people, because there will always be a return on your investment.

A PATTERN FROM SCRIPTURE

God set a pattern we should consider for ourselves. It was given to the tribe in Israel whose members were the only ones who could "work" in the Tabernacle, the Levites, but I think we can learn from it. It's found in Numbers 8:23–26, where at the age of fifty, those guys were supposed to quit working and spend the rest of their years passing on and teaching the younger people what they knew.

That makes sense in that people should, at one point in their life, really concentrate on passing on what they have learned and helping the younger generation learn and do well.

WHAT TO TEACH

Use your Bible as the textbook. *All* of it. It comes from the very breath of God. He is powerful enough to ensure it has remained solid and accurate over all these years. You can rely on it, and you can take any reservations or concerns as to its accuracy and relevance off of the table. Don't fall for any of the lies from Satan about it. (Refer to the previous chapter on "Study.")

Commentaries are good for helping to understand the passage, related and parallel passages, and the context. Other reference materials, articles, blogs, and so on, can be used with discernment, but always use the Bible as your solid main foundational source.

Teaching the Bible to others through topics is one good way. Teaching through a book is another way. Here are more suggestions for what and also *how* to teach:

- For youngsters, teach core topics such as creation from early Genesis, the birth of Jesus, the teaching of Jesus, and the death and resurrection of Jesus.
- For young married couples, teach through the passages addressing the husband, then the wife, and the roles God has outlined.
- For those struggling with sin, teach what sin is, how it has separated us from God, and how Jesus removed that separation. Teach repentance and forgiveness, then hope and a bright future. Use relevant Bible passages to do so.
- Teach how to deal with the issues of life, such as trials from James, what to think about from the lessons of Philippians, what others should see in us from the fruits of the Spirit in Galatians, and the armor of God from Ephesians.
- For the troubled, doubting, and fearful, teach God's promises.
- Teach Jesus' parables. Those are fun and *very* relevant.
- Finally, just answer someone's questions from a biblical perspective.

WHY YOU SHOULD TEACH

God's plan for you is to teach His Word to others, which glorifies Him. Paul, who was probably the greatest teacher ever other than Jesus, says in 2 Timothy 3:16–17 that the Bible is important and even profitable for

- *Teaching*: To cause to know, to know how, to instruct, and to guide. It is to be done regularly.

- *Reproof:* To point out a fault or error in thinking or actions.
- *Correction:* To correct the above error. To bring into conformity with a standard.
- *Training in righteousness:* Outlining the above standard, and methods of following the standard, which is God's truth—the Bible, personified in Jesus.
- *That the man* (the person) *of God may be competent, equipped for every good work:* And that is your goal.

Hebrews 5:12–14 provides an admonishment of spiritual immaturity and lack of growth. It is also why you need to study and to teach the Bible to others:

For though by this time you ought to be teachers, you need someone to teach you again the first principles of the oracles of God; and you have come to need milk and not solid food. For everyone who partakes only of milk is unskilled in the word of righteousness, for he is a babe. But solid food belongs to those who are of full age, that is, those who by reason of use have their senses exercised to discern both good and evil.

In this passage, the writer also implies that you mature in the Word to a point in time where you are to teach it, like a person who graduates from milk to solid food. That means you are to not only teach it but also exercise good discernment in the choices you make daily.

HOW TO TEACH

Start with one person, and work up to more from there. Start also with short passages and progress to topics or larger passages. We get this idea from Ephesians 6:17 (which is the passage on the armor of God), where God's Word is likened to a sword but not just any long sword: it's a special one.

The original Greek word for sword in Ephesians 6:17 is *makhaira*, which is actually more like a two-sided knife, not a large heavy wielding sword. It was about 12 to 18 inches long, and with it, the Romans conquered the world. With specific training, they could defeat their enemy one-on-one by getting in close and precisely delivering a stab.

Paul uses that word makhaira to describe in a word picture that it's best to use and teach God's Word to the one person you are closest to. Also, it's important to do so precisely, after some study or training. This passage adds to that word picture: "For the Word of God is living and powerful and sharper than any two-edged sword, piercing even to the dividing apart of soul and spirit, and of the joints and marrow, and is a discerner of the thoughts and intents of the heart" (Heb. 4:12).

SEQUENTIAL PHASES OF TEACHING

When you teach God's Word to others, please include these three sequential phases of teaching: Knowledge → Understanding → Wisdom.

Are these three words synonyms? Today, most people think so, including teachers, pastors, and parents ... the influential people who *should* know the difference. The distinctness of each and sequential training of all three have been lost, and society today is suffering because of it.

Yes, knowledge, understanding, and wisdom are three different things:

Knowledge is the careful and thorough study of, including memory learning of, things.

1. *Understanding* is how those things work, came about, and are used.
2. *Wisdom* is knowing how to apply these things to what you say or do.

Wisdom is the goal and end result of knowledge and understanding, and it cannot occur without the foundation set by those two. They must occur sequentially. Any statement or task, when done alone or out of sequence, is a disaster, and you don't have to go far to see the carnage. Look at most Facebook comments or letters to the editor or the subject of nightly news reports or even a botched auto repair ...

Prior to doing a brake job on your car, you must read the chapter on replacing brakes in a repair *manual* (or watch a YouTube video), understand how the brake system works, how to disassemble the parts, and how they all go back together. You must even go through the process in your mind, or you will have a disaster. In the nontangible issues in life, the ever-relative and ever-current *manual* is the Bible. So what exactly does it say about knowledge, understanding, and wisdom?

Proverbs 2:6 says, "For the Lord gives wisdom: out of His mouth cometh knowledge and understanding." Couple that with 2 Timothy 3:16, which says, "All Scripture is breathed out by God and profitable for teaching, for reproof, for correction, and for training in righteousness, that the man of God may be competent, equipped for every good work," and you understand that knowledge and understanding, indeed *all* Scripture, has been breathed out of the mouth of God. The Bible is your basis of knowledge and understanding, which God then uses to impart wisdom to us … and *through* us when we teach others.

Jesus expects you to study the Bible (see the previous chapter). Then your confidence to teach it will increase because God promises to give us wisdom from studying it. While this may seem daunting, it really isn't … that's why the Bible is comprised of smaller books and even smaller stories and advice. The book of James, for example, is great little book on advice for living, and it even starts out telling us how to gain wisdom:

> If any of you lacks wisdom, let him ask of God, who gives to all liberally and without reproach, and it will be given to him. But let him ask in faith, with no doubting, for he who doubts is like a wave of the sea driven and tossed by the wind. For let not that man suppose that he will receive anything from the Lord; he is a double-minded man, unstable in all his ways. (James 1:5–8)

Remember in the previous chapter "Study," I mentioned it is good to look at a passage and see what words jump out at you? Those words become pivotal *bam!* words that make the passage relevant to you and to others you teach. In this previous passage, the word "faith" is in the middle and is central to the passage's meaning. In fact, it's the very foundation of the passage. Faith is the key to gaining wisdom, trusting God, and to not doubt. Hebrews 11:6 says without faith, it is impossible to please God. Faith is the key that unlocks the door and lets wisdom from God in.

Doesn't it sound familiar there in James that people without wisdom (from knowledge and understanding) who doubt God and the Bible are like a wave of the sea, driven and tossed by the wind, or are unstable? Most biblical Christians I know are even-keeled and stable. Teach others how to be stable, anchored to God and His Word like a boat anchored in a harbor.

James also says that without faith, you cannot have wisdom. Faith takes effort to get. Paul also wrote in Romans 10:17 that faith comes from learning by reading the Bible: "So then faith comes by hearing, and hearing by the word of God." So read the Bible. The book of James is good, and so is 1 Peter. Then try 1 John. Your life will change for the better when you read those books, and so will the lives of those you instruct.

Since I am in the building industry, I can't resist sharing one more powerful passage. Consider the wisdom of Proverbs 24:3–4: "Through wisdom a house is built; and by understanding it is established; and by knowledge the rooms are filled …"

A stable person is like a house whose foundation is wisdom, framed by biblical understanding, and furnished with biblical knowledge.

Knowledge is not enough; we must apply. Understanding is not enough; we must do. Knowing and understanding in action make for honor. And honor is the heart of wisdom.
—Johann von Goethe

We bring glory to God when we teach His Word as *the* basis for knowledge, wisdom, and understanding. As Solomon said, man's all comes from obeying Scripture. Teach others well!

PRACTICAL APPLICATIONS

1. Whom in your life do you teach? If no one, find someone.

2. _____

    _____

3. _____

    _____

17 WORSHIP

"Give to the LORD, O families of the peoples, Give to the LORD glory and strength.

Give to the LORD the glory due His name; Bring an offering, and come before Him. Oh, worship the LORD in the beauty of holiness!" (1 Chron. 16:28–29)

Giving glory to God is worship! We are made to worship, and worship can be done in many ways. If you have read this book so far, you have learned sixteen ways to bring glory to God. There actually is one more, which embodies all sixteen, weaving them together into what is called *worship*.

Before getting into all of what worship means, take a look at the last part of the passage above. We are to worship the LORD God "in the beauty of holiness!" Holiness or being holy means "set apart." We Christians are set apart from others in the world. A common way of saying this is, "We are in the world, but not of the world." We live life according to biblical principles, not according to the world's system. Our values, morals, focus, and efforts are biblically (life) based, not worldly (perishing) based. And this brings worship to God. When we are biblically holy, it's like we sparkle in the light; we are a *beauty* to others (if they will notice) and beautiful to God!

First Peter 2:9 uses Old Testament concepts to say to you and me, "But you are a chosen generation, a royal priesthood, a holy nation, His own special people, that you may proclaim the praises of Him who called you out of darkness into His marvelous light." I may be myopic, but this seems to indicate we true Christians are the only people who can worship God … and we should take this privilege *seriously*, making worshipping God a *priority*, including doing so *correctly* and *admirably*.

The word "worship" is extremely important, and we need to fully understand its meaning to do so correctly to make it pleasing and acceptable to God. The word "worship" has changed a bit over time, so looking at the original meaning will help us understand how to worship correctly and fully today. Similarly, some other words that have changed over time also come to mind:

Clue was the word for a string of yarn in medieval times where a maze made of corn or hedges was popular. Adults loved to find their way through the maze, then they would run a clue (string line) through the correct route in the hedge maze for children to follow. Nowadays, the word clue doesn't mean a string line; it more connotes bits of information or pieces of evidence.

Naughty comes from the description of very poor people who "have naught (not)" or nothing. Naughty people didn't have much or anything of value. In general, the majority of those people typically resorted to crime or bad choices so, over time, the meaning changed from poor people to immoral people who make bad choices or do illegal things.

Meaning of the word "worship"

To many Christians and Christian churches, worship means singing songs … and that's about all. How wrong that is! It used to mean so much more, and it still does: we just need to be reminded and, for some of us, *educated*!

Worship comes from the old English word *woerthship* or worth-ship. It means to ship out an expression of worth. As we often do, we lazily simplify words, which is sad. That's because the word "worth-ship" reminds us of the meaning better than the simplified word "worship." When you worship God, you are carrying out a highly esteemed, reverent, and respectful expression of the *worth* you have for Him.

That word "worth" is important. God is "worthy." And our endeavor is to express to God how worthy He is to us, honoring His "esteemed value."

I believe the worth of God is infinite, which means we cannot express adequately His worth or, in other words, our inability to worship Him adequately. However, God knows this about us, and He is pleased when we try. So try we must.

I looked up the word "worship" in the dictionary, and from this meaning, I developed a string line (clues) through several words to fully understand the "maze" of this wonderful and important word. Follow these clues with me here:

The dictionary offered one applicable meaning for *worship*: "reverence offered a divine being or supernatural power; *also*: an act of expressing such reverence."[29]

So what does *reverence* mean? I found this: "Honor or respect felt or shown: deference; *especially*: profound adoring awe and respect."[30]

Then I had to look up *deference* because it's a word I have heard, but didn't know the meaning: "Respect and esteem due a superior or an elder; *also*: affected or ingratiating regard for another's wishes."[31]

Esteem I knew, but I also looked that up, just to be sure: "The regard in which one is held; *especially*: high regard."[32]

Well, *regard* means "The worth or estimation in which something or someone is held: a feeling of respect and affection."[33]

Do you have respect and affection toward God?

So to sum it up, worship is the act of expressing reverence, showing profound adoring awe and respect with highly esteemed regard and affection.

As we often do today, I did a Google search of "worship is …" and was blown away by how much there is online in answer to this question. Somewhat surprisingly, it's all good stuff too! There are numerous books written about what worship is, and although I didn't read all of them, I did read several books by John MacArthur, John Piper, and N. T. Wright, and what they say can be boiled down to one simple conclusion: "Worship is giving God His worth."

I came to the realization the amount of *worth* we have to express to God is proportionate to our knowledge and view of Him. That's why knowing God and having knowledge of Him is so important. The prophet Hosea thought this, too, and even wrote down what God said about the matter in Hosea 4:6: "My people are destroyed for lack of knowledge."

Proper worship of God involves understanding as best as we can the awesomeness of God and our posture in that fact. To make this point very clear, approximately forty times in Scripture, when someone worships someone in top authority such as a king, and especially when people actually *do* see God in the future (such as in the book of Revelation), without exception, they *fell down on their faces* and worshipped.

That term "fell down" means they literally were overwhelmed to the point of not being able to stand … they fell to the ground uncontrollably, with their face to the ground as a display of humility or even of being unworthy to be looked upon. Wow. What does that tell you?

Maybe we should consider that posture sometime when we come before Him in prayer.

TRUE WORSHIP COMES FROM A BIBLICAL HEART

True worship comes from a biblical heart. *Heart* is a reference to our innermost being, and a biblical heart means we sincerely

- Repent of our sins, and surrender our life to Jesus and His will
- Serve Jesus as a willing servant (in the positive sense of the word)
- Serve others as Jesus would
- Believe God, and His Word … all of it
- Trust God
- Endeavor to grow spiritually in knowledge and bear "fruit"

Knowledge, mentioned by God in Hosea 4:6, comes from hearing and studying the Word of God, which, like food is to our bodies, is to be done in bite-size pieces each day. Worship is a result of Word study. God's Word is truth, and we are to worship in and from truth.

Jesus talked about worship with the woman at the well in John 4:19–26, and we can learn a lot from Him in this passage. If you know the story, you know Jesus mentioned to her He knew she was not married and had five previous husbands. She quickly changed the subject and did so by instigating what she thought was an argument (or a successful diversion) from a sore subject. Jesus uses this abrupt change in topic to teach her—and us all—what worship really is:

> The woman said to Him, "Sir, I perceive that You are a prophet. Our fathers worshiped on this mountain, and you Jews say that in Jerusalem is the place where one ought to worship." Jesus said to her, "Woman, believe Me, the hour is coming when you will neither on this mountain, nor in Jerusalem, worship the Father. You worship what you do not know; we know what we worship, for salvation is of the Jews. But the hour is coming, and now is, when the true worshippers will worship the Father in spirit and truth; for the Father is seeking such to worship Him. God is Spirit, and those who worship Him must worship in spirit and truth." The woman said to Him, "I know that Messiah is coming [who is called Christ]. When He comes, He will tell us all things." Jesus said to her, "I who speak to you am He." (John 4:19–26)

The first thing we see in this passage is that the woman was confused about worship, or at least she wanted to know where and how to worship properly. We all can relate to this; I think we all are a little confused or have some misconceptions about true worship. We tend to think we can only worship in church, on a certain day of the week, and in one or a few specific ways. Jesus' answer to her basically said that you don't have to go to a specific place to worship.

Second, Jesus said God our Father is seeking worshippers who do so correctly, so it's *acceptable*. This reminds me of a story about a company that manufactured portable CD players. They were hiring assembly workers and selected one hundred applicants to come in at a specific time. All were placed in a room, and each person was given a 3D puzzle in pieces with no instructions and were asked to assemble the puzzle in fifteen minutes. There were fourteen people who correctly assembled the puzzle in the specified time and were accepted for employment. Forty-two people somewhat assembled the puzzle in the allotted time, but they did it incorrectly. They were not hired and sent home as a result.

The fourteen people who got the job either previously knew how to assemble the puzzle correctly or had the desire and intention to figure out the puzzle. Either way, the employer was seeking people who could do what was required on their own—intuitively and correctly. God is seeking worshippers like that.

The third thing we see is to infer there is a false way to worship (a way that's incorrect, does no good, nor goes anywhere) and a true way to worship. Jesus said, "True worshippers will worship the Father in spirit and truth." It is interesting to me Jesus knows there is a wasted way of worship and an acceptable way to worship, and the acceptable way is in spirit and truth.

JESUS TAUGHT US HOW TO WORSHIP.

In the John 4 passage, Jesus said true worship is done in spirit and in truth. Notice Jesus mentions God is Spirit, but He doesn't necessarily *say* the Holy Spirit when He says to worship "in spirit and truth." The spirit He mentions is a brilliant quadruple entendre. Only Jesus is smart enough to use a quadruple entendre (four meanings for one word or phrase, with all four meanings having validity).

- The first meaning of spirit is being like-minded, or of the same beliefs as God: Some would say it's "having a biblical world view." Being sincere in your biblical views is important, since it also means you have a singular frame of mind. Joshua said this in Joshua 24:14 as was giving his final speech near the end of his life: "Now therefore, fear the LORD, serve Him in sincerity and in truth, and put away the gods which your fathers served on the other side of the River and in Egypt. Serve the LORD!" This meaning of spirit is alluded to in the phrase "In the spirit of the laws of this country, this court hereby comes to order."

- The second meaning relates to your mental and emotional disposition or mind-emotion balance, and the best way I can explain it is with the word "fervor." Having "team spirit" comes to mind where everyone has enthusiastic loyalty to their team and a common goal. In high school, we would have a spirit rally to get everyone fired up about winning an upcoming football game. "That's the spirit!" is often said as encouragement to someone who keeps at a task until it's finished, even when it's difficult.

- The third meaning of spirit from Jesus refers to your soul. Worship comes from a righteous standing in our soul … where we are truly saved from the penalty of our sins by repenting of our sins and accepting Jesus as our Savior and Lord. Worship comes from our soul and innermost parts being "right standing" with God through Jesus. We often use the phrase "He has the right spirit to teach that scriptural passage."
- The fourth meaning of spirit is the essence or quality or ingredient that defines the whole. Mixed drinks are called "spirits"—an example would be the spirit (rum) in a Pina Colada. Another would be the spirit in spirit of camphor (ethyl alcohol). So the spirit of you as a Christian is that defining element in you, and one might specifically say that's the Holy Spirit.

Spirit and truth go together here, not one more than the other nor devoid of the other. The conjunction "and" combines the two equally. Consider when worship, including church services, is focused on one more than the other:

- Worship that is too much "spirit" nearly always migrates to be overtaken by emotions pushing out truth. It then becomes organic, unstructured, and frenzied. Jesus becomes friend or lover, diminishing His deity. It resorts to entertainment, which escalates in importance. It also becomes unproductive and unfulfilling, often losing people who want deeper meaning.
- Worship that is too much truth nearly always migrates to be overtaken by the mind, pushing out emotion, and becomes mechanical, rigid, and legalistic. As a result, Jesus becomes deity only, who is not personable. This cerebral worship becomes lofty and cliquish, appearing cold, graceless, and exclusionary, shunning people who cannot "keep up" mentally.

Here is a sketch made during an explanation of this using a metaphor of a pendulum swinging between spirit and truth. An equal balance down the middle is perfect, as Jesus said. Jesus knows how people tend to migrate to one edge or the other and asks us to hang in the middle, using a healthy dose of both to maximize each. It is truly amazing how Jesus knew what He was talking about!

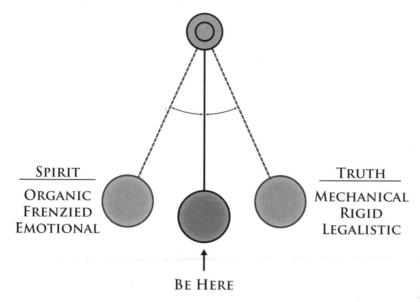

SPIRIT

ORGANIC
FRENZIED
EMOTIONAL

TRUTH

MECHANICAL
RIGID
LEGALISTIC

BE HERE

Worshipping in spirit and truth means they both exist with the help of the other. Not all one and little of the other, not some of one and some of the other. Each is informed by the other. Each relies on the other and is enhanced by the other, and each is even defined most accurately when using the other. Fully Spirit and fully truth.

Want to see something fascinating? Similar to above, when trying to describe Jesus, we say He's both God and man. Not part God and part man, not all God and some of man, nor all man and some of God. He is fully God and fully man. Spirit and Truth! This commonality of descriptions is not a coincidence, worship and Jesus are explicitly linked together!

If you are worshipping so others will see and notice how "spiritual" you are, you are not worshipping God. If you are puffed up by your knowledge of biblical truth and point out to others where they are wrong, you are worshipping what you know and what others perceive about you. You're *not* worshipping God.

If you reflect back to the very beginning of this book, the first few pages hammered home that you don't do these sixteen things to glorify yourself, nor do you do them to gain favor, blessings, or any sort of righteous stand-ing before God. Jesus took care of that for you if you believe. You do these things and worship Him out of love for and adoration of God as a way of giving thanks and expressing worth!

True worship does come from the Holy Spirit, who points us to Jesus and uses His Word (truth) to do that. Therefore, when we are to worship in spirit and truth as Jesus said, the Holy Spirit is there helping us. I think that's part of what Paul talks about in Romans 8:26–27: "Likewise the Spirit also helps in our weaknesses. For we do not know what we should pray for as we ought, but the Spirit Himself makes intercession for us with groanings which cannot be uttered. Now He who searches the hearts knows what the mind of the Spirit is, because He makes intercession for the saints according to the will of God."

True worship not only comes from our actions but also from our best efforts. Thinking our best *of* Him, giving our best *to* Him, and doing our best *for* Him. Whatever we do, we must do heartily (giving our best) to the Lord as Colossians 3.23 says. Doing things for God and for His glory ... that is worship.

True worship is a balance of all the above.

YOUR SENSE OF WONDER

One of my favorite lines in the 1994 Paramount Pictures movie *I.Q.* is when elderly Albert Einstein (played by Walter Matthau) asks easy-going mechanic Ed Walters (Tim Robbins) to find and bring him a prized pos-session from his trousers.

The desirable item is a compass given to Albert by his father when he was young: "When I first held it in my hand, I was wonderstruck ... by what force, invisible and unfelt, could be holding the needle."[34] A some-what confused Ed, still eager to learn from the genius, looks at the old man inquisitively. Then Albert hands Ed the compass for him to keep and tells him this priceless advice: "Here, Edward, you take this ... keep your sense of wonder."[35]

Worship toward the one true God, the creator and sustainer of all that exists—including the purr of a lap cat, the colors of a sunset, the unbeliev-able rock formations in Arches National Park, the untethered moon, the sincere love of a beautiful wife, the warmth of a campfire, the regularity and awe of Old Faithful, or the pull on a compass needle—is not accurate or authentic without a sense of wonder.

Wonder is a feeling of astonishing amazement with exciting admiration a bit of mystery, then having the good sense to leave it right there. Wonder tells God, "I am simple and lowly, but You alone are imaginative, awesome, and beyond my comprehension. Thank you for allowing me to see in part."

I don't think you can worship God correctly without a sense of wonder.

"SO, IS SINGING SONGS WORSHIP OR NOT?"

Of course, singing songs is worship! The Bible tells us a lot about singing songs as worship. Please understand it's one way to worship, but it's not the only way. Singing should certainly be part of your worship repertoire. And please understand this: not all church songs are worthy of worship. In fact, that assessment is often highly subjective based on the content of the lyrics.

This became a topic of this book after my wife and I took our high school-aged daughter to visit Christian colleges she was potentially interested in attending. The student guide at one particular university opened a door to a large building and exclaimed with an enthusiastic grin: "This is where we worship!"

The facility was stunning, with warm colors, comfy seats, ornate wood, stage lighting, three large screens, and a bank of speakers to rival any concert venue. I asked if this was the only place to worship, and our young trendy hipster guide said, "Yes! Isn't it awesome?!"

My wife put her hand on my shoulder in an effort to calm me. (She knows when I am about to unleash the hounds.)

"So, you don't worship anywhere else, only in here?" I asked. My shoulder began to hurt ...

"Yes!" was his reply.

"Why not anywhere else?" I asked, feigning ignorant stupidity.

"Because this is where the instruments and electronics are."

"Dude—" I said to the hipster guide as my wife quickly walked away in abandonment. "Christians can worship other places, too, and it doesn't have to always involve music."

I got no reply, just a look from our hipster guide of utter confusion, or maybe it was I had become a gray-haired zombie to him. We then moved on to the gymnasium …

Worship is expressing worth to God. Again, it *can* involve music, but that's only one way to worship. When we do worship with music, the songs we sing must have lyrics that express the worth of God. The songs we sing should not have "vain repetitions as the heathen do" as Jesus said in Matthew 6:7, so please avoid songs that repeat the same line over and over (especially if it's not biblical).

To be a true worship song, there must be at least one of the elements of glorifying God in the lyrics. Here are some examples:

- Prayers sung to God should follow the manner of praying Jesus taught in Matthew 6. These songs are rare; however, because prayer by definition is your personal conversation with God. You may do that in the form of music, but it's rarely done in corporate church singing.
- Faith, hope, and love are three elements of glorifying God, so if those are woven into the lyrics, it makes for a great worship song!
- Abiding in Jesus, obeying Him, and acknowledging Him are also elements of a wonderful worship song.
- Words of thanks is a theme of some of my most favorite worship songs—thanking God for what He has done, is doing, and will do.
- Praise is probably the most popular worship song theme. These songs praise God for who He is and usually center on some of His attributes and holiness.
- Worship songs that are theologically rich and accurate are timeless worship songs. These lyrics teach us biblical truths, enrich and edify us with God's Word, and are even a way to memorize Scripture. Several old hymns are rich with biblical truth, and I love to sing them. We can dwell on Scripture richly with songs, especially when we can sing the tune in our head throughout the day.

When searching the Bible for passages about singing as worship, I discovered three key themes: First, singing songs is always a form of worship in the Bible. Second, there is an entire book in the Bible dedicated to singing songs. So singing must not only be an important part of living the Christian life, but pPsalms is a song book that is "theologically rich!" Third, several places in Scripture mention three types of singing as worship: singing psalms, hymns, and spiritual songs. Those three must be different types of ways to glorify God through singing.

So here is what I think:

- *Singing psalms*. This must mean exactly what it is: singing one of, or part of, the lyrics from the book of pPsalms.
- *Hymns*. These are songs written by people. They follow a pattern of music, such as four stanzas with a chorus. Think of opening a hymnal in church and singing along with everyone. This is called corporate worship through hymns.
- *Spiritual songs*. These are often made-up songs or some modern worship or praise songs you primarily sing yourself. They are spiritual, biblical, and include one or more of the elements of how to glorify God.

Here are my two favorite passages about singing as worship. I noticed a few things when studying them. See if you notice them too:

"Let the word of Christ dwell in you richly, teaching and admonishing one another in all wisdom, singing psalms and hymns and spiritual songs, with thankfulness in your hearts to God" (Col. 3:16).

"And do not get drunk with wine, for that is debauchery, but be filled with the Spirit, addressing one another in psalms and hymns and spiritual songs, singing and making melody to the Lord with your heart" (Eph. 5:18–19).

- Notice that songs are a means of letting the Word of Christ dwell in us richly; that's why it's important for the lyrics to come from the Bible (Word of Christ).
- In addition to that, notice that the song lyrics are to teach us all biblical wisdom.
- Notice as well that these songs are also designed to admonish us in all wisdom. Admonish means to warn or to notify of a fault or to counsel against wrong practices. Song lyrics must do that.

- Notice a theme of these passages and the words "addressing one another" as songs build each other up.
- Notice the songs must have or create in our hearts thankfulness to God. This is a joyous attitude of appreciation and praise, like a delightful melody.
- Since the Bible and specifically Jesus is the source of all wisdom, the lyrics must be from the Bible and Jesus to correctly accomplish those tasks in the song.
- Notice we are to be filled with the Spirit when addressing one another in songs and not act like we are drunk when singing.
- Notice the Ephesians passage adds the words "making melody to the Lord with your heart." I think God appreciates a song with a good melody. Those are delightful, and they create a wonderful "vehicle" for expressing, learning, and admonishing God's Truth.
- Notice "to God" and "to the Lord with your heart." This simply means that songs are a way to glorify God!

Singing songs as a way of worship is found throughout the Bible, so it must be throughout your life too!

THE RECIPE OF WORSHIP

Worship is worth-ship. So how do we take the *worth* God is to us and *ship* it off to Him? There are sixteen ways, or sixteen ingredients, that together make up wholesome worship, much in the same way a good chef mixes the ingredients of the entree at your favorite restaurant and sends the product to your table:

- Praying often
  - Use all four types of prayer: formal, ritual, flare, and spontaneous.
- Having faith and hope
  - We live by faith which comes from reading the Bible, not seeing and reacting to what's around us. Faith pleases God because His word governs our life, not the world's "system."
- Love (both God, and one another)
  - All of God's requirements of us hinge on love.

- Abide in Jesus
  - True Christians live—and gain all strength, nourishment, and direction—from Jesus. That's how you produce fruit, which is the first command given.
- Obedience to Him
  - Live inside the "Big O" of obedience. It's better there, and life is abundant there!
- Acknowledge Him in all you do
  - Live according to knowledge … of Him. Relate all of life to Him.
- Living with integrity
  - When your biblical beliefs dictate your actions, you live in integrity. And you stand out as light in darkness, so people will rise and call you blessed.
- Being skillful in what you do
  - Be the best and most skilled _____ (fill in the blank) in your whole town. Your witness depends on it because you will be noticed by all people, even leaders.
- Being a godly and positive influence on others
  - Let God's light shine through you like through a diamond against black velvet. This allows you to make an impact for Him where He has placed you and to the people He has placed around you.
- Being like a mirror image of Jesus
  - A person fully alive in Jesus is a glory to God.
- Enduring the troubles and suffering in this life with a godly attitude and perspective
  - Don't let life's occurrences dictate your theology. Remain tethered to your anchor (God), and peace will rule your life. Your witness depends on it.
- Being thankful
  - And that means being thankful in *everything*! You can always find something to be thankful for, so thank God for what He's done and remember those blessings. The more thankful you are, the more you will have to be thankful *for*!

- Praising God in several different ways. Singing is only one of them!
  - Praise God for who He is and how He has shown you His awesome attributes.
- Being generous and giving sacrificially
  - God owns everything. You decide how much of His you want to keep … your theology dictates how generous you are, and your attitude depends on it.
- Study God's Word
  - You get sixteen things when you study God's Word … all life's abundances come from studying and doing. Remember: location, location, location …
- Teach God's Word, and these ways to glorify and worship Him
  - Knowledge … wisdom … understanding. These are sequential and important to life. You learn best when you teach. There are people who are depending on you.

Worship is a lifestyle … is it *yours*?

Worship is the most powerful, joy producing, hope sustaining, life altering thing we do.
—Pastor Dr. James MacDonald

As a final thought, I can only think of nothing better than to quote the best God-glorifier I know of … the apostle Paul, who wrote in Romans 11:36, "For of Him and through Him and to Him are all things, to whom be glory forever. Amen."

NOTES

1. The Westminster Shorter Catechism, 1647
2. John Wayne (Marion Robert Morrison) 1907–1979 American Actor.
3. George Muller (1805–1898) Christian evangelist and director of the Ashley Down orphanage in Bristol, England. https://chatna.com/george-muller-quotes/
4. *Merriam-Webster Online, s.v.* "faith," https://www.merriam-webster.com/dictionary/faith.
5. Bodie Hodge, "How Long Did It Take for Noah to Build the Ark?" Answers in Genesis. June 1, 2010. https://answersingenesis.org/bible-timeline/how-long-did-it-take-for-noah-to-build-the-ark/.
6. *Merriam-Webster Online, s.v.* "service," https://www.merriam-webster.com/dictionary/service.
7. Ibid.
8. These quotations are from The Holy Bible, New International Version. Grand Rapids: Zondervan House, 1984. Print.
9. Duramax is a trademark of General Motors Company.
10. *Merriam-Webster Online, s.v.* "integrity," https://www.merriam-webster.com/dictionary/integrity.
11. Henry Cloud, *Integrity* (New York: Harper Collins, 2006).
12. WordHippo.com, s.v. "skill," https://www.wordhippo.com/what-is/the-meaning-of-the-word/skill.html.

13. Ibid.

14. Ibid.

15. Os Guinness, *The Call* (Nashville: W Publishing Group, 1998).

16. *Merriam-Webster Online, s.v.* "image," https://www.merriam-webster.com/dictionary/image.

17. James Strong, *Strong's Exhaustive Concordance of the Bible* (Nashville: Abingdon Press, 1890).

18. Charles Stanley, *Advancing through Adversity* (Nashville: Thomas Nelson, 1996), eBook.

19. Oswald Chambers, *My Utmost for His Highest* (Oxford, UK: Alden Press, 1924), 177.

20. http://www.abrahamlincolnonline.org/lincoln/speeches/thanks.htm

21. *Merriam-Webster Online,* s.v. "praise," https://www.merriam-webster.com/dictionary/praise.

22. *Merriam-Webster Online*, s.v. "bless," https://www.merriam-webster.com/dictionary/bless.

23. *Oxford Dictionaries*, s.v. "service," https://www.lexico.com/en/definition/service.

24. Ibid.

25. David Jeremiah, Shadow Mountain Community Church www.shadowmountain.org www.davidjeremiah.org

26. Fred R. Shapiro and Joseph Epstein, *The Yale Book of Quotations* (New Haven, CT: Yale University Press, 2006).

27. Scripture quotations marked "ESV" are from the The Holy Bible, English Standard Version®), copyright © 2001 by Crossway, a publishing ministry of Good News Publishers. Used by permission. All rights reserved.

28. *Merriam-Webster Online, s.v.* "sound," https://www.merriam-webster.com/dictionary/sound.

29. *Merriam-Webster Online, s.v.* "worship," https://www.merriam-webster.com/dictionary/worship.

30. *Merriam-Webster Online, s.v.* "reverence," https://www.merriam-webster.com/dictionary/reverence.

31. *Merriam-Webster Online, s.v.* "deference," https://www.merriam-webster.com/dictionary/deference.

32. *Merriam-Webster Online, s.v.* "esteem," https://www.merriam-webster.com/dictionary/esteem.

33. *Merriam-Webster Online, s.v.* "regard," https://www.merriam-webster.com/dictionary/regard.

34. https://en.wikipedia.org/wiki/I.Q._(film)

35. http://www.script-o-rama.com/movie_scripts/i/iq-script-transcript-albert-einstein.html